SCREEN ADAPTATIONS
SHAKESPEARE'S
KING LEAR
THE RELATIONSHIP BETWEEN TEXT AND FILM

YVONNE GRIGGS

methuen | drama

In memory of Big Al, The California Man

1 3 5 7 9 10 8 6 4 2

First published in Great Britain in 2009 by Methuen Drama

Methuen Drama
A & C Black Publishers Limited
36 Soho Square
London W1D 3QY
www.methuendrama.com

Copyright © Yvonne Griggs 2009

Yvonne Griggs has asserted her rights under the Copyright, Designs and
Patents Act, 1988, to be identified as the author of this work

A CIP catalogue record for this book is available from the British Library

ISBN 978 1 408 10592 4

Printed and bound in Great Britain by
CPI Cox & Wyman, Reading, Berkshire

contents

preface

....

King Lear is considered one of Shakespeare's greatest tragedies. It has been adapted in vastly different ways over the last four centuries by fellow dramatists, novelists, and film and television screen writers. Though seen initially as a means of lending artistic weight to the cinematic medium in its infancy, screen adaptations of Shakespeare's plays have continued to thrive; their sheer volume suggests that the stories they tell and the issues they raise are still of interest to contemporary audiences. *King Lear* proves to be no exception to the continuing trend.

This book focuses specifically on feature-length cinematic adaptations of *King Lear*, ranging from those considered to be part of the canon of Shakespeare on screen, to its art house reconfigurations, and various mainstream genre interpretations of the play. Discussion is divided into sections according to film type (canonical *Lears,* genre cinema *Lears,* art house *Lears*) and focuses on the influences at work in each film's adaptive transition from play text to screen. The status of the 'classic' literary text and each of its cinematic counterparts is considered in relation to current debates on Shakespeare on screen. Traditional, outmoded discourses related to textual 'fidelity' and overworked auteurist readings of the adapted film text are counter-balanced by the introduction of new genre-focused ways of reading canonical screen versions of *King Lear*, historically neglected genre versions, which have remained outside the critical fold for far too long, are also given close critical attention.

There are a number of adaptations of *King Lear* which were produced for television. BBC versions were televised in 1948, 1982, and 1998, Richard Eyre's production with Ian Holm being the most recent rendition. Thames TV aired a production of the play starring Patrick McGee as Lear in 1976, and in 1983 an ageing Laurence Olivier was cast as Lear in Granada Television's *King Lear*. However, although More4's Nunn/McKellen *King Lear*, televised in December 2008, forms part of the discussion of the play's 'afterlife', the decidedly cinematic rather than tele-visual preoccupations of this study preclude detailed exploration of such adaptations.

acknowledgements

I would like to express my thanks to various institutions that have helped me to access copies of films, screenplay drafts and shooting scripts, some of which proved extremely difficult to track down. The Folger Library, the BFI and the British Library have all come to my aid during the course of my research.

I am also indebted to my De Montfort University colleagues. My thanks are extended to Imelda Whelehan and Ian Hunter for their guidance and encouragement throughout the lengthy research process, and a special note of gratitude goes to my editor, Deborah Cartmell, for both her tireless support and her constructive critiques of the work in progress.

Permissions
The author and Methuen Drama are grateful to the following publishers for their permission to use the following.

'Dogmatic Shakespeares: A "Recognition of Ghostly Presences" in Thomas Vinterberg's *Festen* and Kristian Levring's *The King is Alive*', *Journal of Adaptation in Film and Performance*, Intellect (vol. 2.2, 2009).

'*King Lear* as Western Elegy', *Literature/Film Quarterly*, Salisbury University, Salisbury, MD 21801 (vol. 35.2, 2007, pp.92–100).

'*King Lear* as Melodrama', *Literature/Film Quarterly*, Salisbury University, Salisbury, MD 21801 (vol. 35.2, 2007, pp.101–107).

'On the Road: Reclaiming *Korol Lir*', *Literature/Film Quarterly*, Salisbury University, Salisbury, MD 21801 (vol. 37.2, 2009, pp.97–108).

'"Humanity must perforce prey upon itself like monsters of the deep": *King Lear* and the Urban Gangster Movie', adapted from the original essay, which appeared in *Adaptation*, Oxford Journals, Oxford University Press (vol. 1.2, 2008, pp.121–139).

'*Ran*: Chaos on the "Western" Frontier', *Journal of Adaptation in Film and Performance*, Intellect (vol. 1.2, 2008, pp.103–116).

timeline: cinematic adaptations of *King Lear*

··

King Lear

1909:	USA
Director:	William V. Ranous
Production company:	Vitagraph

King Lear

1910:	Italy
Director:	Gerolamo Lo Savio
Production company:	Film d'Arte Italiana

King Lear

1916:	USA
Director:	Ernest C. Wade
Production company:	Thanhouser Film Corporation

House of Strangers

1949:	USA
Director:	Joseph Mankiewicz
Production company:	Twentieth Century Fox Film Corporarion

Broken Lance

1954:	USA
Director:	Edward Dmytryk
Production company:	Twentieth Century Fox Film Corporation

Korol Lir
1970:   Soviet Union
Director: Grigori Kozintsev
Production company: Lenfilm Studio

King Lear
1971:   UK
Director: Peter Brook
Production company: Athéna Films

The Godfather
1972:   USA
Director: Francis Ford Coppola
Production company: Paramount Pictures

The Godfather: Part II
1974:   USA
Director: Francis Ford Coppola
Production company: Paramount Pictures

King Lear
1976:   UK
Director: Steve Rumbelow
Production company: British Film Institute Production Board

The Dresser
1983:   UK
Director: Peter Yates
Production company: Goldcrest/World Film Services

Ran
1985:   USA
Director: Akira Kurosawa
Production company: Greenwich Film Productions

King Lear

1987:	USA
Director:	Jean-Luc Godard
Production company:	Cannon Films

The Godfather: Part III

1990:	USA
Director:	Francis Ford Coppola
Production company:	Paramount Pictures

A Thousand Acres

1997:	USA
Director:	Jocelyn Moorhouse
Production company:	Touchstone Pictures

The King is Alive

2000:	Denmark/Sweden/USA
Director:	Kristian Levring
Production company:	Newmarket Capital Group

My Kingdom

2001:	UK
Director:	Don Boyd
Production company:	Close Grip Films Ltd.

PART 1:
Literary contexts

'The wheel is come full circle': origins and new directions

••

Recycled narratives

King Lear draws upon an amalgamation of existing narratives, and has been interpreted as both a redemptive morality tale and a vision of apocalyptic doom. Throughout its performance history, it has been constantly reworked and radically edited to realise interpretations that suit the mood and values of its contemporary production climate.

The tale of King Lear and his daughters is one that has become part of the literary landscape of Western culture, and the skeleton of the narrative is familiar to many. At its most basic level, *King Lear* tells the story of a monarch who has tired of the demands of leadership and, consequently, decides to relinquish governance to his daughters, who must 'earn' their share of his kingdom by performing public declarations of their love for him. It is the youngest and most favoured daughter's refusal to comply with his request, and Lear's petulant response to her refusal, that sets the narrative in motion. Goneril and Regan (and their respective husbands, Albany and Cornwall) assume control of Lear's divided kingdom; Cordelia, having disobeyed her father and voiced her doubts about the sincerity of her sisters' love for him, is exiled along with Lear's trusted adviser, Kent. From this point onwards Lear's powers diminish whilst those of his remaining daughters increase. Throughout the course of the narrative we witness his mistreatment at the hands of Goneril and Regan, his physical disintegration, his descent into insanity, and his ultimate redemption in the play's closing moments as he is reconciled with the exiled Cordelia. *King Lear's* subplot serves to amplify the play's exploration of the roles of fathers and their offspring. Gloucester is easily duped, his fatherly love and trust misplaced; yet, like Lear, he eventually learns the error of his ways. For many, *King Lear* is a tale of moral redemption: by journeying through the depths of despair and emerging as a man who is ready to acknowledge and learn from his mistakes, Lear exemplifies the possibilities of Christian forgiveness. However, the very dark and violent undertones embedded within Shakespeare's verse also invest the text with a less hopeful message. Lear, the man, may be 'saved' but humanity is still left to 'prey upon itself,/Like monsters of the deep' (4.2, 50–51).[1] Law and order are seemingly restored but we doubt both its longevity and humankind's capacity to reject greed and corruption, or to refrain from acts of cruelty.

The many narratives from which Shakespeare's *King Lear* borrows are less well known. These range from the play's basic affiliation to fairy tales concerning fathers and daughters, to the populist historical account of King Leir found in Holinshed's *Chronicles*. The plot line of the *Lear* story is particularly similar to that of the fairy tale,

[1] William Shakespeare, *King Lear*, The Arden Shakespeare, 3rd edition, ed. R.A. Foakes (London: Thomas Nelson & Sons, 1997). This edition has been consulted as it gives details of both Quarto (1608) and Folio (1623) texts; it indicates where passages appear in one text but not in the other, and thus provides the reader/adapter with the opportunity to explore all performance possibilities. Unless stated, all further passages from *King Lear* are taken from this edition.

'The Goosegirl at the Well': in this fairy tale, a king asks his three daughters to declare their love for him, and the size of their inheritance is decided in accordance with the measure of their love. Whilst the elder daughters acquiesce, delivering lines which please their egotistical father, the third fails his 'love test'; she claims that she loves her father 'like salt', since 'the best food does not please (her) without (it)'.[2] But such a claim is considered an inadequate expression of love, and she is cast out by her petulant father who learns to repent as the tale unfolds.

In addition to the similarities shared with such fairy tales, Shakespeare's play builds upon the historical narrative of King Leir, first recounted in Geoffrey of Monmouth's *Historia Regum Britanniae* (c. 1135), and retold by Raphael Holinshed in *The Chronicles of England, Scotlande and Irelande* in 1587. Though commonly viewed as historical accounts, both have greater affinities with folklore and mythology than with fact. In Geoffrey's account, the love test and the allocation of dowries revolves around the brokerage of marriages for all three of Leir's daughters; the story concludes with the suicide of Cordeilla, who, after restoring her father to the throne, succeeds him, only to be overthrown and imprisoned by her nephews. Holinshed's version follows a similar narrative and both writers focus on the civil wars that ensue, the Dukes of Albany and Cornwall leading the attack against Leir.

As an adapter, Shakespeare refocuses the narrative lens, moving us away from the warring factions at the heart of earlier historical accounts and towards a closer examination of the protagonists at the centre of the story. *The Mirror for Magistrates*

---

[2] 'The Goosegirl at the Well', *The Baldwin Online Children's Literature Project* (2000–2008). Online: www.mainlesson.com/display.php?author+hunt&book=grimm&story=well

(1574, Folios 47–54, 211–217) relates in poetic form 'The Trageodye of Cordila', detailing her desperation as a result of her imprisonment by her nephews:

> In spiteful sorte, they used then my captive corse,
> No favour shewde to me, extinct was mine estate.
> Of kindred, princesse bloud, or pere was no remorce,
> But as an abject vile and worse they did me hate,
> To lie in darksome dungeon was my fate.

In a final act of desperation, and prompted by the ghost of 'Despaire', Cordila commits suicide. Edmund Spenser's *The Faerie Queene*, 1590 (Book II, Canto 10, 27–32), also traces the history of King Leyr and envisions Cordelia's death by hanging:

> So to his crown she him restored againe,
> In which he dyde, made ripe for death by eld,
> And after wild, it should to her remaine:
> Who peaceably the same long time did weld:
> And all mens harts in dew obedience held;
> Till that her sisters children, woxen strong
> Through proud ambition, against her rebeld,
> And ouercommen kept in prison long
> Till wearie of that wretched life, her selfe she hong.

But it is not until Shakespeare's version of events that her hanging is tranformed from an act of suicide to one of murder, ordered by Edmund, son of Gloucester, who enters the story line as part of a subplot grafted onto the *Lear* narrative. The subplot introduced by Shakespeare allows for further illumination of the main plot's examination of filial love and matters of loyalty.

Nevertheless, whilst inventively woven into the play's overriding themes by Shakespeare, it too is a story line which has, in part, been appropriated from elsewhere. Sir Philip Sidney's *Arcadia* (1590) tells of a blind Paphlagonian king, deceived by his illegitimate son, Plexirtus, yet saved by his other honourable and legitimate heir, Leonatus. Robert Greene's *Selimus,* published in 1594 and relocating events to early sixteenth century Turkey, replaces daughters with sons in a tale of political intrigue and filial wrongdoing, this time perpetrated by the youngest son who murders both his father and his siblings. Notions of filial duty, of disloyalty and sibling rivalry resonate throughout this text and Shakespeare's *King Lear.*

However, it is the anonymous *True Chronicle History of King Leir,* published in 1605 but performed from 1594 onwards, that most closely resembles Shakespeare's tale of fathers wronged by their offspring. Richard Knowles notes 'almost one hundred details common to these two plays but found in virtually none of the other sources'.[3] In both we have dead queens, and kings who wish to 'Unburdened crawl toward death' (1.1, 40); the details of the reconciliation scenes between Cordelia and Lear are also strikingly similar. Yet one text emerges as an iconic work of literature of tragic proportions, whilst the other remains a relative unknown, consigned to the realms of 'pleasant historical romance'.[4] The extent to which Shakespeare was familiar with this, the only other contemporaneous, dramatic reworking of the *Lear* story line, remains debatable, but his knowledge of it and of numerous previous renditions of the Lear story cannot be denied. In the true spirit of the inventive, creative adapter, Shakespeare owns the

[3] Richard Knowles, 'How Shakespeare Knew *King Lear*', in *Shakespeare Survey: 55, King Lear and its Afterlife,* edited by Peter Holland (Cambridge: Cambridge University Press, 2002), p. 14.

[4] Ibid., p. 13.

version he eventually distils; he recycles the narratives and plays with the thematic concerns explored in existing texts. Most significantly, his text owes nothing to its predecessors in terms of its versification and dramatic realisation.

Considerations of textual 'fidelity' are further complicated by the existence of several posthumously generated substantive versions of Shakespeare's *King Lear*, none of which can be categorically regarded as the definitive text. Kiernan Ryan notes that the Quarto of 1608 and the Folio of 1623 share no fewer than eight hundred and fifty verbal variants; furthermore, he questions, firstly, whether either represents a 'reliable transcription of the script as performed by Shakespeare's company', and secondly, whether we can be sure that Shakespeare was involved in the editing of the 1623 Folio.[5] Whilst the textual solution for some editors has been to bring elements of the two texts together to produce a conflated version,[6] others have adopted a bi-textual approach. The 1986 Oxford edition, printing both Quarto and Folio versions side by side, claimed rather contentiously, that 'for the first time, *King Lear* is printed both as Shakespeare originally wrote it and as he revised it, some years later in the light of performance',[7] despite the difficulties of proving that either text represents conclusively what Shakespeare originally wrote or later revised.

However, this search for a definitive text has become of far more concern to readers of the text than to those involved in its production on stage or screen, and remains an anathema to the

[5] Kiernan Ryan, '*King Lear*: A Retrospective, 1980–2000', in *Shakespeare Survey: 55, King Lear and its Afterlife*, edited by Peter Holland (Cambridge: Cambridge University Press, 2002), pp. 2–3.

[6] Ibid., p. 3.

[7] Stanley Wells and Gary Taylor, eds, *The Complete Oxford Shakespeare* (Oxford: Oxford University Press, 1986).

film industry because of the collaborative and financially-driven nature of film's production processes. Renaissance scholar Allardyce Nicoll, writing in 1936, points out that, in Elizabethan and Jacobean times, the work of Shakespeare and his contemporaries was similarly collaborative and financially constrained: their creative output 'once paid for by the management, ceased to be their property, might be used in any way that that management saw fit and was not *likely* to view the light of day in printed form'.[8]

'This great stage of fools': *King Lear* in performance

First performed in 1606, Shakespeare's tragedy emerges as a play which, unlike those of his contemporaries or his own earlier tragedies, subverts the tragedic conventions of the genre, moving away from the accepted formulaic elements of Greek tragedy and into new dramatic territory. In the creative spirit of adaptation, the convergence of certain elements of the aforementioned texts and Shakespeare's own narrative and linguistic interventions result in a rendition of Lear's tale that is marked out as being different to its predecessors in both content and form. Resisting a connection to any geographical or chronological framework, *King Lear* builds instead upon the narrative's mythical properties and, throughout its performance history, has continued to accommodate the cultural and social preoccupations of each production era. Shakespeare's play is, like its screen successors, a form of adaptation, constructed from a range of existing narratives that have not only evolved over time but in response to the more pressing concerns of each production's 'moment'.

[8] Allardyce Nicoll, *Film and Theatre* (London: Harrap & Company Ltd, 1936), pp. 2–3.

During the course of the last four hundred years, Shakespeare's plays have been amended and interpreted to suit the mood of contemporary production. Nahum Tate's 1680 version of *King Lear* became the accepted version of 'Shakespeare's' play for over a century, despite the liberties taken with the text's story line and its thematic preoccupations. The morally ambiguous elements of the text were eliminated, tragi-comic moments were cut, and a romantic liaison between Cordelia and Edgar was inserted to ensure restoration of order, resulting in a long series of productions which – in addition to omitting central characters like the Fool and radically altering the narrative outcomes – had no qualms about operating outside what is often ambiguously termed the 'spirit' of the source text. The preference for Restoration comedies and its aversion to the play in its Shakespearean form reflected the period's unwillingness to engage with some of the fundamental questions it raises. It was not until the era of the Romantics that Shakespeare's version of the *Lear* narrative regained prominence. By 1838 the melodramatic leanings of Tate's adapted text were excised; William Charles Macready's *King Lear* reintroduced the Fool and restored Shakespeare's tragic ending, Tate's version becoming a 'derisory footnote to the history of the masterpiece'.[9] Macready's heavily edited rendition played to its Victorian audience's desire for spectacle, and again in response to Victorian taste, later cuts reflected Victorian sensibilities, with Gloucester's blinding being removed from Henry Irving's 1892 *King Lear*.

[9] Peter Womack, 'Secularizing *King Lear*: Shakespeare, Tate and the Sacred', in *Shakespeare Survey: 55, King Lear and its Afterlife*, edited by Peter Holland (Cambridge: Cambridge University Press, 2002), p. 96.

Dominant readings of *King Lear*: a tale of redemption or fall?

King Lear is one of Shakespeare's most complex texts, presenting a range of themes for exploration on both stage and screen. Its concerns are often cited as universal and timeless, its locale seen as being open to a multitude of interpretations. Similarly, its chameleon-like properties mean that its dominant thematic preoccupations vary from one stage or screen production to another, depending upon the interpretation adhered to. The failure of patriarchal institutions, at both a familial and a political level, and the play's examination of the boundaries of sanity, its obsession with identity crises revolving around issues of masculinity and the redundancy of language are of central importance. However, whilst some productions emphasise humanity's relentless march towards the apocalypse, or focus on the repressed sexual energies at work within patriarchal institutions in general and the family in particular, others focus on the redemptive path travelled by King Lear during the course of the narrative. Productions also present us with contrasting approaches to the characterisation of Lear. He can be the misguided, 'foolish, fond old man' (4.7, 60) who 'hath ever but slenderly known himself' (1.1, 294–295), and who is constructed ultimately as victim. Or he can be the dictatorial 'dragon' (1.1, 122), instrumental in his own downfall and capable of casting out – 'Unfriended, new adopted to (his) hate,/Dowered with (his) curse and strangered with (his) oath' (1.1, 204–205) – those who choose to question his wisdom.

Critical response to the play is also vast and varied. In the first half of the twentieth century criticism was dominated by redemptive readings of the text associated with a Christian value system. A.C. Bradley saw it as a play of 'reconciliation',[10] whilst G. Wilson Knight,

[10] A.C. Bradley, *Shakespearean Tragedy: Lectures on Hamlet, Othello, King Lear and Macbeth*, 2nd edition (London: Macmillan, 1905).

writing in the thirties, considered it a purgatorial text in which redemption is earned through a process of purification;[11] more than twenty years on, these sentiments remained part of the critical landscape in some academic circles. However, though considered by many to be a regenerative morality tale – Cordelia functioning as agent of her father's redemption – such readings were also challenged during this era, most notably by Jan Kott whose bleak, nihilistic interpretations of the text filtered into the performance, leading to productions that highlighted the absurdity and the apocalyptic propensities of existence. 'The theme of *King Lear* is the decay and fall of the world', according to Kott,[12] and Peter Brook's highly influential RSC production, staged in 1962, encapsulated Kott's bleak interpretation of the work. Kiernan Ryan notes a decided shift of critical thought from this point onwards:

> In the 60s the Christian paradigm that had governed criticism of the play for most of the century was displaced by two new critical dynasties: on the one hand upbeat humanist views of the tragedy as vindicating the value of human suffering; on the other the downbeat conceptions of *King Lear* as Shakespeare's *Endgame*, a vision of existence as a brutal, pointless joke.[13]

Critical thought in the eighties began to focus on issues relating to gender, language and power[14] rather than matters of redemption or annihilation. Marxists, cultural materialists and new historicists

---

[11] G. Wilson Knight, *The Wheel of Fire: Interpretations of Shakespearean Tragedy* (London: Methuen, 1949).

[12] Jan Kott, *Shakespeare Our Contemporary* (London: Routledge, 1967), p. 120.

[13] Ryan, p. 1.

[14] Ibid., p. 2.

'polariz(ed) around the politics imputed to the text', whilst feminist critics were divided, reading the play either as reflective of 'a patriarchal bard' or, conversely, as a 'critique of misogynistic masculinity'.[15] For Coppélia Kahn, for example, it is a play about masculinity in crisis;[16] for Kathleen McLuskie, it remains a misogynistic text in which human nature is defined as 'explicitly male', and women are defined only in terms of their gender, sexuality, position within the family and resistance to their father: they are saints or sinners whilst Lear is the much maligned patriarch.[17] The play's inherent contradictions continue to invite a destabilising array of contradictory ideological positions, and the existence of both a Quarto and a Folio edition of the text further exacerbates its innate instability.

The adaptation debate

Historically, the adaptation debate has been dominated by academics working from a literary bias, resulting in the inevitable favouring of literary source texts, the artistic merit and independence of the resultant screen adaptations being superseded by their origins. Whether approaching the concept of adaptation from a theoretical or a practical perspective, the problems related to the term and its application continue to flourish, especially when

[15] Ibid., p. 7.

[16] Coppélia Kahn, 'The Absent Mother in *King Lear*', in *Rewriting the Renaissance: the Discourses of Sexual Difference in Early Modern Europe*, edited by Margaret W. Ferguson, Maureen Quilligan and Nancy Vickers (Chicago: University of Chicago Press, 1986), pp. 33–49.

[17] Kathleen McLuskie, 'The Patriarchal Bard: Feminist Criticism and Shakespeare: *King Lear* and *Measure for Measure*', in *Political Shakespeare: New Essays in Cultural Materialism*, edited by Jonathan Dollimore and Alan Sinfield (Manchester: Manchester Univeristy Press, 1985), pp. 90–99.

the waters are clouded by the additional consideration of a source text's literary status. Shakespeare's plays, whether destined for either stage or screen, are afforded such iconic status within contemporary Western culture that to be seen to tamper with them in any way is to provoke anguished cries of protest from Shakespeare 'purists' who seek fidelity to the text above artistic freedoms at production level.

According to R.A. Foakes, attempts to 'free performance from the bondage of texts' constitute a misguided desire to escape the authority of Shakespeare.[18] Yet there are theatre practitioners and academics who take a very different stand in the adaptation debate. Charles Marowitz believes that the only way to overcome 'the deplorable, anal retentiveness of the canon'[19] to which Shakespeare and other writers of classic literary texts have been confined, is to adopt a 'Quantum Leap Approach'[20] to adaptation, creating works which radically transpose rather than reproduce the original. Robert Stam views the process of adaptation as part of a continual process of textual recycling,[21] one which Linda Hutcheon cites as a 'creative and interpretive act of appropriation' or 'salvaging'.[22] Shakespeare's plays are themselves shaped by such interpretive acts of appropriation or salvaging. Moreover, Douglas Lanier argues that populist adaptations (labelled 'Shakespop' by Lanier) which engage in a 'wider array of interpretive positions vis-à-vis the

[18] R.A. Foakes, 'Performance Theory and Textual Theory: A Retort Courteous', *Shakespeare* 2.1 (2006), p. 47.

[19] Charles Marowitz, *Recycling Shakespeare* (London: Macmillan, 1991), p. 15.

[20] Ibid., p. 9.

[21] Robert Stam, 'Beyond Fidelity: The Dialogics of Adaptation', in *Film Adaptation*, edited by James Naremore (London: The Athlone Press, 2000), p. 66.

[22] Linda Hutcheon, *A Theory of Adaptation* (New York & London: Routledge, 2006), pp. 8–9.

Shakespeare works they engage',[23] encourage a dialogue with their Shakespearean predecessors that returns his work to their rightful place in the 'long tradition of imitation and adaptation from which their status as literary monuments has tended to isolate them'.[24]

Many structural taxonomies have been generated by adaptation theorists – from Geoffrey Wagner to Dudley Andrew, or Michael Klein and Gillian Parker[25] – but there remains no clear consensus of opinion as to which of them, if any, should be regarded as definitive, leaving us with a range of strategies to adopt as a means of analysing the resulting adaptations. Furthermore, Thomas Leitch notes that the desire to employ the kind of classifications put forward by these theorists and their successors (Kamilla Elliott, John Desmond and Peter Hawkes, Linda Cahir)[26] may provide the field of adaptation studies with a more clearly defined theoretical territory, but it also ensures – to the detriment of fruitful academic debate – the continuance of value judgements: adaptation theorists continue to 'define (the) field with

[23] Douglas Lanier, *Shakespeare and Modern Popular Culture* (Oxford: Oxford University Press, 2002), p. 88.

[24] Ibid., p. 85.

[25] Geoffrey Wagner, *The Novel and Cinema* (Cranbury: Associated University Press, 1975); Dudley Andrew, *Major Film Theories: An Introduction* (London: Open University Press, 1976); Michael Klein and Gillian Parker, *The English Novel and the Movies* (New York: Frederick Ungar, 1981).

[26] A range of alternative classifications are expounded in the works of these theorists: Kamilla Elliott, *Rethinking the Novel/Film Debate* (Cambridge: Cambridge University Press, 2007); John Desmond and Peter Hawkes, *Adaptation: Studying Film and Literature* (Boston, Ma: McGraw-Hill, 2006); Linda Costanzo Cahir, *Literature into Film: Theory and Practical Approaches* (Jefferson, NC: McFarland, 2006).

primary reference to its closeness to literature'.[27] However, pre-occupation with the author and *the work* is a relatively recent development.[28] Such preoccupations would have had no validity in Elizabethan and Jacobean times when writers like Shakespeare were adept in the art of borrowing the ideas of other authors; the very notion of a stable work by the author, Shakespeare, would have been alien in this age and borrowing seen as an age-old accepted means of creating. As late as the eighteenth century, the freely adapted performances of Shakespeare's plays often bore little resemblance to the stabilised textual versions which had established themselves by the Romantic period;[29] but whilst Shakespeare as text divorced from Shakespeare as theatre has become acceptable, and theatre is now regarded as 'high' culture despite its initial status as entertainment for the masses, Shakespeare as film is still unable to attain a similarly independent stature.

New critical studies of not only the resulting adaptations but of the processes and cultural forces at work in their conception and production do much to lead us away from entrenched debates revolving around issues of fidelity to a so-called 'primary source' text. Work in the field of adaptation by Deborah Cartmell and Imelda Whelehan shifts the focus of academic discussion consider-ably from a literary framework to one which adopts a cultural studies framework, focusing on a cultural studies approach that 'foregrounds the activities of reception and consumption' rather than outmoded debates concerning the 'cultural worthiness' of

[27] Thomas Leitch, 'Adaptation Studies at a Crossroads', *Adaptation* 1.1 (2008), p. 64.

[28] André Bazin, 'Adaptation or the Cinema as Digest', in *Film Adaptation*, edited by James Naremore (London: The Athlone Press, 2000), p. 23.

[29] Graham Holderness, *Visual Shakespeare: Essays in Film and Television* (Herts: University of Hertfordshire Press, 2002), p. x.

either the film adaptation or its literary source text.[30] Building on this cultural studies approach in their recent publication, *The Cambridge Companion to Literature on Screen*, Cartmell and Whelehan define literary texts as 'intertexts' as opposed to 'primary sources', and argue that literary texts form just a part of a 'multiplicity of perspectives' at work in the creation of the screen adaptation.[31] Issues related to the film industry's production climate are also becoming an increasingly important part of the debate.[32]

Film is a highly collaborative process relying on collective creative energies. However, to the detriment of open debate, film scholars and Shakespeare scholars alike continually strive to retain the primacy of 'authorship', the director invariably usurping the role of writer and in this instance becoming a pseudo-Shakespeare. Attempts to establish the primacy of auteur-driven adaptations of Shakespeare's plays in turn generate a questionable, elitist hierarchy of screened Shakespeare that manufactures a discrete body of film work deemed canonical (and thus worthy of critical consideration), and a body of screen adaptations that fall outside the parameters of the canon and into a critical no-man's land. Graham Holderness notes that *certain* academics have been instrumental in what he terms the disconcerting 'canonical

[30] Imelda Whelehan, 'Adaptations: The Contemporary Dilemmas', in *Adaptations: From Text to Screen, Screen to Text*, edited by Deborah Cartmell and Imelda Whelehan (London and New York: Routledge, 1999), p. 18.

[31] Deborah Cartmell and Imelda Whelehan, 'Introduction – Literature on Screen: a Synoptic View', in *The Cambridge Companion to Literature on Screen*, edited by Deborah Cartmell and Imelda Whelehan (Cambridge: Cambridge University Press, 2007), p. 3.

[32] Emma French, *Selling Shakespeare to Hollywood: The Marketing of Filmed Shakespeare Adaptations from 1989 to the New Millennium* (Herts: Hertfordshire Press, 2006).

appropriation' of *certain* screen adaptations of Shakespeare's plays by a select number of auteurist filmmakers.[33] The works of Roger Manvell, Charles Eckert, Jack Jorgens and Anthony Davies are cited as crucial to the establishment of a 'particular canon of great films by great directors – Olivier, Welles, Kozintsev, Kurosawa, Brook'[34] creating an elitist hierarchy within the field of screened Shakespeare studies, in which 'the circle of greatness'[35] becomes set by these influential academics to the exclusion of other screen adaptations, especially, it would seem, those seen to operate firmly within the realms of genre cinema.

Kenneth Rothwell's invaluable work as historian of cinematic Shakespeare has helped to shape the critical landscape; similarly, Davies is credited with shifting the focus of discussion of film from the textual into the realms of the visual and the spatial.[36] Peter Donaldson also opens up new, psycho-analytical pathways into the critiquing of screen Shakespeares. But all such readings continue to view the films from either a Shakespearean standpoint, seeking out parallels with the source text and its stage renditions, and identifying ways in which the verse is realised in cinematic space as opposed to theatrical space, or from an author-dependent, auteurist standpoint that purposely invests the film with the same kind of aesthetic weight as the source text. The focus moves away from consideration of film text or, indeed play text, as a product destined for a specific market place, and can inadvertently lead once more to reductive, fidelity-conscious readings of the films under review. It appears that by focusing on

[33] Holderness, p. 70.

[34] Ibid., pp. 69–70.

[35] Ibid., p. 69.

[36] Anthony Davies, *Filming Shakespeare's Plays: The Adaptations of Olivier, Welles, Brook and Kurosawa* (Cambridge: Cambridge University Press, 1990).

the artistic credibility of the film's creator – highlighting *en route* their theatrical leanings – these academics are trying to force the inception of a filmic hierarchy in which the film can establish its high art status alongside that of the source text. Elsie Walker suggests that the current critical preoccupation with auteurist readings of screened Shakespeare precludes other discursive possibilities; in seeking to replace the authorial expressivity of Shakespeare with that of the auteur, the debate returns to tired issues of fidelity, the director credited as auteur serving as a culturally acceptable replacement for Shakespeare.[37]

At a conceptual level, genre provides an alternative critical framework that highlights the intertextual relationship between the Shakespearean source text and the resultant screen adaptation, moving us away from the traditionally auteur-driven readings of screened Shakespeare, away from reductive fidelity issues, and from the well-trodden path of establishing parallels between film text and play text, screen space and theatrical space. Yet existing scholarship pays little heed to the significance of genre frameworks. This study employs a genre framework to the reading of film adaptations of *King Lear*, thus bringing both canonical and genre-based reconfigurations into the critical fold for the first time. The narrative of *King Lear* contributes to and is reproduced in a range of film genres. It is reincarnated in existing screen versions in genre forms as diverse as the western, the *film noir*, the gangster, melodrama and road movie. Even its art house rebirths are open to genre classification as a specific type of product operating within a loose set of predetermined conventions. Some of the re-workings

---

[37] Elsie Walker, 'Getting Back to Shakespeare: Whose Film is it Anyway?' in *A Concise Companion to Shakespeare on Screen*, edited by Diana E. Henderson (Malden, Oxford, Victoria: Blackwell Publishing, 2006), p. 13.

of the *Lear* narrative, of both art house and more mainstream generic leanings, may have a less overt relationship with Shakespeare's play than others, but they are no less a part of the adaptive landscape than traditional canonical adaptations. Moreover, in the case of screen versions of *King Lear*, it is difficult to cite films that operate within the realms of the traditional; even those films deemed canonical can be read as genre products, or are of such an experimental nature that they find no place alongside the more conservative Shakespearean screen adaptation. The latter type of adaptation retains both the narrative structure and the versification of its source text; it conforms to expectations of mainstream cinematic language, invariably adopts a lavish costume drama approach in which production values and visual spectacle take precedence over creative interpretation, and its adherence to 'fidelity' becomes its guiding – often its *misguiding* – light.

Screen Shakespeare remains shadowed by fidelity debates, despite the considerable inroads made by adaptation theorists over the years. Harry Keyishian claims that when the plays are made into films, it is Shakespeare's work that must adapt to the authority of film rather than film that must adapt to the authority of Shakespeare.[38] Courtney Lehmann echoes this sentiment stating that where cinema once turned to Shakespeare for 'cultural legitimacy' it is now Shakespeare that needs cinema for its 'cultural longevity'.[39] Yet Cartmell highlights the continuing prejudice surrounding the field of screen adaptations which source literary classics: 'film purists' are seen to be as antagonistic towards the

[38] Harry Keyishian, 'Shakespeare and the Genre Movie: The Case of *Hamlet*', in *The Cambridge Guide to Shakespeare on Film*, edited by Russell Jackson (Cambridge: Cambridge University Press, 2000), pp. 73–81.

[39] Courtney Lehmann, *Shakespeare Remains: Theatre to Film, Early Modern to Postmodern* (Ithaca and London: Cornell University, 2002), p. 235.

adaptation of literary works to screen as those 'literature purists' who bemoan the raiding of literary classics by the film industry.[40] By employing genre as a conceptual prism through which to explore the relationship between Shakespeare's *King Lear* and the varied array of film adaptations it continues to generate, this study aims to widen the circle of debate, replacing value judgements based on notions of literary and auteurist pedigree or that of the medium of expression, with meaningful discussion about the intriguing inter-textual connections established during the *process* of adaptation from text to screen.

[40] Deborah Cartmell, 'Film as the New Shakespeare and Film on Shakespeare: Reversing the Shakespeare/Film Trajectory', *Literature Compass* 3.5 (2006), p. 1152.

PART 2:

Production contexts

From play text to silver screen

Screen *Lears*: an overview

From the early days of cinema to the present day, the hybridity of Shakespeare's plays has assured them a continued screen presence, though the agenda behind their appropriation varies, reflecting the contemporary film production climate. There are currently an estimated 700 films and TV productions, including genre adaptations, which are indebted to Shakespeare for their origins,[1] and echoes of Lear's story continue to resonate throughout visual media of both 'high art' and populist leanings.

Since, in its formative years, cinema was ostensibly viewed as a low-brow form of entertainment for the masses, an infusion of Shakespeare was seen as a means of 'civilizing the hordes' who attended the populist nickleodeons.[2] A number of silent screen adaptations of *King Lear* appeared between 1909 and 1916: the Vitagraph's one-reel version was released in 1909, followed by an Italian *King Lear* in 1910, and a Thanhauser production in 1916. In

 [1] Daniel Rosenthal, 'The Bard on Screen', *The Guardian*, 7 April, 2007.

[2] Kenneth Rothwell, *A History of Shakespeare on Screen: A Century of Film and Television*, 2nd edition (Cambridge: Cambridge University Press, 2004), pp. 4–7.

recent times, the commercial film industry's attempts to redefine Shakespeare as both popular *and* artistic have resulted in a rash of productions in the 1990s which sought mass market appeal through a reshaping of Shakespeare's plays into popular generic forms.[3] Though successfully reconfigured into a variety of popular cinematic genres since the forties – the first gangster *noir*, *House of Strangers*, appearing in 1949 – *King Lear* is one of few Shakespeare plays that has remained decidedly resistant to relocation into the teen mass market. Its ageing protagonist is, it seems, of limited appeal to the contemporary teen-dominated multiplex audience.

Writing back in the mid eighties, Neil Sinyard noted the play's capacity to 'strike a particular chord with twentieth-century sensibilities,' its ability to 'speak to the moral chaos and confusion of our time'[4] affording it a special affinity with a century associated with the horrors of two world wars and a host of apocalyptic possibilities. However, despite this and its continuing contemporary concerns – the dysfunctional family, the failure of patriarchal institutions, humanity's relentless march towards the apocalypse – there have been relatively few feature length screen adaptations of the play. From the mid-twentieth century onwards, there are only six populist genre reworkings of the text, the most recent of which (*My Kingdom*) was released in 2001. Furthermore, there is a conspicuous absence of art house and/or canonical cinematic versions of *King Lear* before the 1970s.

Traditionally, critical debate hinges around consideration of the canonised versions of *King Lear* on screen: Grigori Kozintsev's *Korol Lir* (1970), Peter Brook's *King Lear* (1971), and Akira Kurosawa's *Ran*

[3] Douglas Lanier, 'Shakespeare and Cultural Studies: An Overview', *Shakespeare* 2.1 (2006), pp. 228–248.

[4] Neil Sinyard, *Filming Literature: The Art of Screen Adaptation* (London: Croom Helm, 1986), pp.18–19.

(1985) are the mainstay of scholarly discussion. There are also a number of inventive cinematic offshoots which attract considerable academic attention: Peter Yates (*The Dresser*, 1983), Jean-Luc Godard (*King Lear*, 1987), and Kristian Levring (*The King Is Alive*, 2000) use the play text as a source of inspiration, selectively employing elements of its narrative and its language. Although widely different in many respects, these canonical and art house adaptations share a resistance to the kind of period drama treatment so frequently realised in screen versions of Shakespeare's other tragedies. And whilst many adapters persist in their pursuit of a screened Shakespeare that employs Shakespearean verse as its vehicle of expression, whether within a period or modern context, it is not until 1971, with the advent of Brook's nihilistic *King Lear*, that Shakespeare's language is transposed to a feature length screen version of this play. With the exception of a very stilted costume drama, directed by and starring Brian Blessed in 1999, it remains the only feature length film of *King Lear* to retain the Shakespearean verse so far.

The screen adaptations of Brook and Kurosawa embrace the loss of faith in narrative progress explored in Shakespeare's text, each envisioning the kind of apocalyptic closure seen by Sinyard as a reflection of modern times. Godard's *King Lear* supposedly takes place within a post-apocalyptic world and explores a similarly down beat reading of the play. Conversely, both Kozintsev and Levring create film texts which explore the redemptive potential embedded in Shakespeare's play: tellingly, they are the only screen *Lears* which offer us the prospect of any kind of salvation.

Unlike genre cinema, art house products revel in their capacity to exude uniqueness and thus to acquire an aesthetic that is seemingly denied the genre-specific film. Yet, somewhat ironically, Shakespeare's plays are characterised by their hybridity, their reliance upon established narrative forms and their initially populist intent, despite their author's posthumously acquired iconic status. Genre-based adaptations of the *Lear* narrative highlight their genre affiliations over and above any overt affiliation with Shakespeare's play. They employ character frameworks and narrative patterns from Shakespeare's *King Lear*, but they also make fascinating ideological and thematic connections with the play text. The long-established tradition of genre reworkings of *King Lear* consists of Joseph Mankiewicz's *noir*-influenced *House of Strangers* (1949), Edward Dmytryk's western *Broken Lance* (1954), Francis Ford Coppola's American gangster trilogy, *The Godfather Parts I, II* and *III* (1972,1974, 1990), Jocelyn Moorhouse's melodrama *A Thousand Acres* (1997), and Don Boyd's British gangster film *My Kingdom* (2001).

The *Lear* story line translates with particular ease to a western or a gangster genre, presenting us with an essentially male-centred quest revolving around the Everyman figure of Lear, and operating within a macho, territorially-driven society. Films following this generic style construct a Lear-like protagonist whose downfall is a consequence of his own actions. However, the play also lends itself to a diametrically opposed realisation as female-centred melodrama. Jane Smiley's novel, *A Thousand Acres*, presents a harsh revisionist reading of the *Lear* text from the perspective of Lear's wronged daughters, but Moorhouse's cinematic treatment translates novel and play into cinematic melodrama. And whilst Kozintsev's *Korol Lir* revolves around the male-centred quest of the king, the redemptive journeying that is so central to this screen translation aligns it with the ideological preoccupations of Moorhouse's female-centred film rather than decidedly male-dominated genre versions like *Broken Lance* or *Ran*. Kozintsev's king, like the women at the centre of Moorhouse's melodrama, emerges as a victim, a 'poor, infirm, weak and despised old man' (3.2, 20) who is 'more sinned against than sinning' (3.2, 60). Both ways of working with the text's classic story are sustainable, and demonstrate not only the hybridity of Shakespeare's play but the inventiveness and commercial acumen of the writers/directors who choose to place this well-known tale into different yet familiar cinematic frameworks. Arguments surrounding the possibilities of successfully translating Shakespeare's verse to the cinema screen may continue to rage, but there is little doubt that Shakespeare's narratives provide malleable story templates which translate to celluloid with ease.

In its earliest genre reincarnations, the *Lear* story line is driven by the preoccupations of its protagonists – Gino Monetti from *House of Strangers*, Matt Devereaux from *Broken Lance*. Unlike the canonical versions of the seventies and eighties, these films concern themselves mainly with personal politics rather than wider issues of significance to humanity. In both gangster readings of the seventies which appropriate elements of Lear's story, and in post-eighties genre versions, any directorial desire to address the 'bigger' issues of existence are jettisoned in favour of a return to a more personalised treatment of the narrative, matters revolving around the concerns of each film's central character: Don Michael Corleone, Ginny, Sandeman.

The changing face of *King Lear*

King Lear has been produced within an incredibly diverse range of contexts. Screen adaptations cover cinemas of various nationalities and product types, from government-funded Soviet cinema to Japanese cinema; experimental British, French and Danish cinema, to US Hollywood films emerging from the Studio System. Michael Anderegg's astute identification of two types of Shakespearean film adaptation succinctly polarises the two potential ends of the production spectrum. Those 'made from the centre' are seen to combine Shakespeare's cultural authority with 'institutional support' of a commercial nature (major studio), governmental nature (Grigori Kozintsev's *Gamlet*, 1964, and *Korol Lir*, 1970) or both (Olivier's *Henry V*, 1944).[5] Actor-directors like Laurence Olivier and Kenneth Branagh provide a type of 'official Shakespeare' which propagates a certain kind of 'Britishness' and as such links Shakespeare to matters of national identity.[6] But *King Lear*'s transition to screen is marked by its resistance to forms that invest the tale with any sense of 'Britishness': instead, it translates with ease to a number of national cinemas and Hollywood studio productions.

Despite being dependent on Western funding of 10.5 million dollars, provided by Serge Silberman, Akira Kurosawa's *Ran* retains a decidedly Eastern aesthetic; Shakespeare's *King Lear* is one of a number of intertexts employed in Kurosawa's retelling of a Japanese legend set in a very specific feudal Japan. Similarly, though Kozintsev's *Korol Lir* openly declares its affiliations with Shakespeare's play, the resultant film text is coloured by the Soviet ideologies of its director and its state sponsors. *King Lear*'s Hollywood mutation to the western frontier, to various mobster underworlds and to a contemporary Iowa farming community further demonstrates its cinematic resistance to affiliation with *any* one geographical, cultural, or historical period, or to any particular mode of industrial production.

At the other end of the spectrum there are what Anderegg terms 'marginal films' which operate outside the realms of the commercial or the governmental, and challenge Shakespeare's cultural supremacy. Welles' films are cited as examples of these marginal

---

[5] Michael Anderegg, 'Welles/Shakespeare/Film: An Overview', in *Film Adaptation*, edited by James Naremore (London: The Athlone Press, 2000), p. 161.

[6] Ibid., p. 162.

adaptations which do not share the same tone of respectability.[7]
Peter Brook's adaptation of *King Lear* (1970), though accepted as
part of the canon of screen Shakespeare, seems to be a film made
'at the margins' rather than 'from the centre', even though it
appropriates Shakespeare's language and is the work of a director
who, like Olivier and Branagh, is undeniably a part of the theatrical
fraternity, as are many of his film cast. His screen adaptation entails
no sense of national identity, of 'Britishness', and presents a fragmentary take on the narrative, employing low budget strategies
that stand in opposition to the high production values of many
adaptations of filmed Shakespeare. His is an experimental piece of
cinema which, whilst emerging from the same production era as
Kozintsev's *Korol Lir*, is influenced by a very different cultural, social,
political and financial production climate.

Whilst Brook shares Kozintsev's desire to create a version of *King
Lear* which rejects the trappings of heritage and Hollywood, their
interpretation of the play differs considerably as does their mode of
cinematic expression. Brook's earlier stage version of *King Lear*
(performed by the RSC in 1962) and his screen adaptation share
his nihilistic reading of the play text – a reading which is clearly
influenced by the writings of critic Jan Kott and by the politics of
the moment, including the aftermath of two world wars and the
ongoing conflict in Vietnam. Furthermore, Brook's *King Lear* is unlike
all other screen adaptations of Shakespeare's plays of this era:
those of his contemporaries conform to heritage genre expectations and embrace the epic grandeur of the 'big screen'.[8] His *Lear*

---

[7] Ibid., p. 161.

[8] Franco Zeffirelli's realist versions of *The Taming of the Shrew* (1966) and *Romeo
and Juliet* (1968), Tony Richardson's *Hamlet* (1969), Stuart Burge's *Julius Caesar*
(1970), and Roman Polanski's *Macbeth* (1971) remain period pieces which conform
to the expected conventions of film practice in a way that Brook's film does not.

and his earlier films[9] belong to a decade of decidedly 'pessimistic (British) cinema' spanning the mid-sixties to the mid-seventies.[10]

Films of an experimental nature similar to that of Brook's *King Lear* can also be seen as operating from the 'margins'. The film products of New Wave filmmakers Jean-Luc Godard and Kristian Levring may emerge from different new waves and different production eras but they share a distaste for all things 'Hollywood'. Jean-Luc Godard, one of the pioneers of the French New Wave back in the late fifties, and Kristian Levring, one of the founders of the Danish Dogme New Wave formed in the nineties, adopt a decidedly experimental approach to the reconfiguration of *King Lear*. Given the nature of Godard's work, it is surprising to find that funding for his *King Lear* came from the mainstream Cannon Group, renowned as producers of eighties genre cinema with a focus on action film products.[11] The mainstream commercial credentials of the Cannon Group seem at odds with the cinematic leanings of a director like Godard, and tensions between the two permeate the film text. Godard's relentless mockery of his backers becomes an intrinsic part of his film text, his anti-Hollywood sentiment playing out on screen as part of an elaborate revenge on his financiers.

Levring adopts a similar position in relation to the Hollywoodisation of cinema. As part of the Dogme New Wave's ideology, Levring seeks a revitalisation and a democratisation of the film industry by challenging Hollywood's global domination of film. The so-called Dogme brethren aim to realise this by releasing film from what they see as the 'technological tyranny' and financial facism of Hollywood,

[9] Brook directed *Lord of the Flies* (1963), *Marat/Sade* (1967), and *Tell Me Lies* (1968).

[10] Robert Murphy, *Sixties British Cinema* (London: BFI, 1992), p. 4.

[11] In the eighties Cannon produced *Texas Chainsaw Massacre II* (1986), *Superman IV: Quest for Peace* (1987), and *The Barbarians* (1987).

giving filmmakers the freedom to operate beyond the confines of big budget production.[12] However, the brethren take a somewhat tongue-in-cheek stance to their New Wave posturing, neither acknowledging nor denying its function as a means of providing a novel marketing platform for their film, and despite the anti-American sentiment of the Dogme New Wave manifesto, Levring's *The King is Alive* was largely dependent on American funding.

Hollywood studio versions of the *Lear* narrative, *House of Strangers* and *Broken Lance*, produced in the forties and fifties respectively, are now regarded as adaptations of *King Lear* but it is difficult to ascertain whether this was ever a conscious, inter-textual appropriation of certain elements of the *Lear* narrative and archetypes, or whether this has been posthumously attached to the films. Contemporaneous reviewers do not make any overt reference to the intertextual connections between Shakespeare's play text and each of these films, and yet in later years, with the advent of DVD releases and their accompanying DVD commentaries, inferences are drawn to convincing and intriguing effect.

The numerous gangster-related re-workings of the *Lear* narrative suggest its close affinity to the gangster movie, and there is an undeniable connection between the theatrical genre of tragedy, especially in its Elizabethan and Jacobean realisations, and the cinematic gangster genre. Seminal gangster movies of the thirties – *The Public Enemy* (1931), *Little Caesar* (1931), and *Scarface: The Shame of the Nation* (1932) – mirror the downfall of the charismatic, Machiavellian anti-hero of certain Elizabethan and Jacobean tragedies. However, the moralistic tone of the gangster film, epitomised by these early gangster classics, became less pronounced as censorship abated, leading to a much more

---

[12] 'Dogme Manifesto', *Dogme95*. Online: www.dogme95

ambivalent realisation of the gangster hero by the late sixties – one which accommodates the creation of mobster patricians of Learesque complexity such as Francis Ford Coppola's Corleones (*The Godfather* trilogy) or Don Boyd's Sandeman (*My Kingdom*). Coppola's films are big budget Paramount studio productions whilst Boyd's *My Kingdom* is a small scale British film released at the height of the British gangster genre's renaissance towards the end of the twentieth century, but both explore to telling effect their affinity with *King Lear* within their respective gangster underworlds.

Jocelyn Moorhouse's star-studded Hollywood realisation of Jane Smiley's *A Thousand Acres* reconfigures both Smiley's novel and Shakespeare's play as melodrama, operating convincingly within a mainstream genre framework for a pre-ordained 'women's weepie' audience far from the realms of its source texts. Yet despite its stellar cast the film was deemed both a critical and a commercial failure, grossing only eight million dollars during its release,[13] and being condemned by film critic Roger Ebert as 'an ungainly, undigested assembly of "women's issues", milling about within a half-baked retread of *King Lear*'.[14]

At the turn of this century, Levring's *The King is Alive* and Boyd's *My Kingdom* entered a market place already saturated with adaptations of Shakespeare's plays. By the end of the nineties, popular genre forms of Shakespeare's texts, ranging from costume drama to teen romance to action film, had been adopted by film-makers in pursuit of what Lanier terms a 'legitimis(ation)' of mass market appeal.[15] The trend continued with films like *O* (2001)

[13] *The Internet Movie Database*. Online: www.imdb.com

[14] Roger Ebert, '*A Thousand Acres*', review, *Chicago Sun-Times*, 19 September, 1997.

[15] Lanier, *Shakespeare*, pp. 228–248.

delivering a high school take on *Othello*, whilst the most recent release, *She's the Man* (2006), adapts *Twelfth Night* into a teen rom-com. The industry's faith in the increasingly mainstream market-ability of such genre versions of Shakespeare is underlined by the latter film's release strategy: it opened on 2623 screens in the USA,[16] an unprecedented number for a product affiliated with Shakes-peare and its 'high art' leanings. Even films which retain the Shakes-pearean verse, such as Michael Almereyda's *Hamlet* (2000), seek a more teen-friendly turn to the narrative, Almereyda casting Hamlet as a much younger man preoccupied with both his love interest, Ophelia, and his angst-ridden dalliance with death.[17] As a play text, *King Lear* retains its distance from teen-screen adapta-tion, but its affiliation with different types of genre cinema and *avant-garde* film continues to flourish.

New ways of reading screen *Lears*

Since *King Lear* is reconfigured in such diverse generic forms, the relationship between film and literature proves particularly revealing in any consideration of film adaptations of this play. Generic criticism may still be regarded by some academics as an imprecise and debased art which is incapable of providing an aesthetic reading of film text, but Leo Braudy's work in the area of genre studies highlights its significance as a 'highly democratic' and 'unifi(ying) cultural force'.[18] If applied to the study of screen Shakespeare, a genre-based approach can free us from what can

[16] Figure from *The Internet Movie Database*. Online: www.imdb.com
[17] Ethan Hawke's Hamlet is a 'media-savvy' loner; Julia Stiles' Ophelia embodies teen audience appeal through her performances in teen Shakespeares (*Ten Things I Hate About You*, 1999, and *O*, 2001).
[18] Leo Braudy, 'Film Genres' in *Film Theory and Criticism: 6th edition*, edited by Leo Braudy and Marshall Cohen (Oxford: Oxford University Press, 2004), pp. 657–662.

be reductive comparisons with the specifics of the so-called 'source' text, allowing us to transcend auteur bias and to study these films from a perspective that not only emphasises their relationship with genre cinema, but considers them in terms of their place within cinematic trends and movements which are in themselves a response to contemporary society and contemporary modes of production. Film theorist Thomas Schatz identifies two distinct mainstream genres: the genre of order (or 'determinate space')[19] includes the western, science fiction, action, and gangster film; the genre of integration (or 'indeterminate space') encompasses such films as the road movie, the musical, the melodrama. Schatz's classifications provide a generic framework against which we can measure the various generic versions of celluloid Shakespeare, generating new ways to 'read' these film texts in relation to their thematic and ideological patterning as well as their audio-visual motifs.

[19] Thomas Schatz, 'Hollywood Genres: Film Genre and Genre Film', in *Film Theory and Criticism: 6th edition*, edited by Leo Braudy and Marshall Cohen (Oxford: Oxford University Press, 2004), pp.691–702.

PART 3:

Readings of key versions

From the canon to Hollywood

East meets West: *King Lear* and the canon

There are three clearly delineated cinematic adaptations which are regarded as canonical readings of *King Lear*: all three are the work of noted auteurs and all are viewed as works of 'high art', their author/directors functioning here as pseudo-Shakespeares. However, two of these three film texts have been claimed – even hijacked – by academia and 'high culture' at the expense of their more populist genre leanings and intent, whilst the experimental nature of the third film is too often overlooked.

Grigori Kozintsev's *Korol Lir* (1970) is the most traditional reconfiguration of *King Lear* to date. It is of classic story design; it presents a consistent reality, deals in linear time, and focuses on the redemptive elements of the narrative to construct an aged Everyman Lear whose quest takes him on a journey of self-discovery.

Kurosawa's *Ran* works through subversion of the culturally specific jidai-geki genre,[1] and the western, epic and horror traditions of

---

[1] The jidai-geki epic belongs to an historically specific and distinctly Japanese period known as the Edo era (1600s–1867). It is often associated with glorification of the samurai and its masculine codes.

Western cinema; even though we are led to an ambiguous, apocalyptic ending rather than the kind of expected closure associated with these more mainstream genre templates, the film's narrative patterning mirrors classic story design in terms of its linear treatment of time, causality and the creation of a consistent reality. Hidetora's 'quest', like that of Kozintsev's *Lir*, shapes the narrative's momentum. Although historically defined as canonical film texts, each of these films exploits elements of mainstream genre convention to creative effect; and it is their inherent if unacknowledged association with the road movie and western/epic respectively that ensures their mainstream accessibility, despite their status as foreign language films within the English-speaking market place.

Peter Brook's film text realises similarly close narrative connections to Shakespeare's *King Lear*. In all three canonical renditions of the play we have an ageing, autocratic patriarch who wilfully (and with limited success) relinquishes control to his less than trustworthy offspring; we have the loyal, initially favoured child whose refusal to pander to a father's whims results in exile; we have a country on the brink of chaos as a result, and the unfolding of the once powerful leader's downfall. And yet Brook's cinematic treatment of this narrative differs considerably, making his adaptation a very different cinematic experience. As with Kurosawa's *Ran*, the ultimate demise of Lear (and by inference of humanity) is the driving force behind this adaptation, but it is Brook's experimental cinematic style that sets it apart from other canonical *Lears*. It inhabits the territory of the art house film product, distorting the narrative to creative effect, yet it retains its storytelling cogency and its identity as an adaptation of Shakespeare's *King Lear*, the psychology of its tragic hero rather than the cause and effect momentum of the classic story design forming the focus of this film in typical art house fashion.

As a means of exploring the influences at work in the adaptive process and the very different ways in which each adapter/director transposes *King Lear* to screen, consideration of each film will include a close cinematic reading of its opening moments.

Peter Brook's King Lear *(1971): 'A Hollywood showman's nightmare?'*

Peter Brook's cinematic vision of *King Lear* is far from the realms of conventional adaptations of Shakespeare on screen. Despite his continuing success as a stage director, his approach is that of the experimental film-maker rather than the theatrical practitioner and his choices are influenced by the conventions of film rather than stage. For Brook, 'the medium is the message'[2] and when operating within the very different creative realm of screened Shakespeare he adopts experimental counter-cinematic techniques more readily associated with the work of the French New Wave than with theatrical practices or cinematic genre renditions of Shakespeare's works. Writing at the time of the film's release, critic Jonathan Raban claims that the film is 'a riot of inexplicable artiness',[3] seemingly a 'Hollywood showman's nightmare';[4] however, Brook's 'artiness' is far from artless and if the film is 'a Hollywood showman's nightmare' one could argue that Brook has achieved his desired effect.

Initially, Brook's adaptation was conceived as a translation: poet Ted Hughes, commissioned to write the screenplay, treated the play text almost as a 'foreign classic'.[5] However, Brook then chose to reassemble the play; returning to Shakespeare's verse for his

[2] Michael Billington, *'Tierno Bokar'*, review, *The Guardian*, 2 June, 2005, p. 26.

[3] Jonathan Raban, *'King Lear'*, review, *New Statesman*, 30 July, 1971.

[4] Jack Jorgens, *Shakespeare on Film* (London: Indiana University Press, 1977), p. 244.

[5] Roger Manvell, *Shakespeare and the Film* (London: J.M. Dent & Sons, 1971), p. 137.

dialogue, he wrote two distinctive shooting scripts. Yet the final screen version is strikingly different from either of these scripts in many respects, suggesting that textual tensions and uncertainties were resolved in response to collaborative on-set production processes rather than during the more solitary process of scriptwriting. All of the action revolves around a dominant, patriarchal Lear whose relationship with his 'wronged' daughters takes centre screen from the outset of the film. The play's subplot is immediately sidelined: we have no sense of Gloucester as a similarly domineering father-figure, nor any indication of Edmund's motivations since the opening dialogue involving Gloucester, Kent and Edmund is cut, as are Edmund's later soliloquies. Gloucester is constructed as a frail old man rather than an astute 'politician'; Edmund, devoid of motivation, emerges as a symbol of the corruption at the heart of Lear's kingdom, whilst Edgar, despite defeating his brother, is denied his moment of glory in the closing moments. Brook shifts the narrative emphasis from the fight between Edgar and Edmund, which is dealt with in a perfunctory manner, to the on-screen deaths of Lear's daughters, and the film ends as it begins, with Lear dominating the frame. Lear's journey is not envisaged as one of redemption but of annihilation: the fragile hope offered at the end of Shakespeare's play does not form part of Brook's narrative.

In this *King Lear*, as the story is transposed to celluloid, Brook's editing and cinematography become arguably as eloquent as Shakespeare's verse. The apocalyptic visions at the core of *King Lear* are accentuated by Brook: he explores the protagonist's internal conflict as a projection of catastrophe, mirroring the late sixties preoccupation with apocalyptic fears. The resultant film text shares with Crisis Cinema a sense of the absurd, and of the diminishing powers of patriarchal systems leading, according to

Christopher Sharrett, to a 'profound nullity and bankruptcy',[6] a nullity that is reflected in the intentional bankruptcy of the on-screen images constructed by Brook. This apocalyptic reading of the text sees Lear slipping out of the frame at the close of the film, leaving us with a blank, white screen held for four seconds. The 'nothingness' at the core of the narrative is given an on-screen reality, suggesting that human life is insignificant and inconsequential. The closing dialogue of the source text is cut and all forms of life seem to be extinct: we are left waiting, anticipating what will come next, but the screen remains blank.

His directorial intent has been debated at length by critics, some condemning him for concentrating upon the text's nihilistic elements to the exclusion of the redemptive properties inherent in Shakepeare's play,[7] whilst others claim it is a film which 'offers more Beckett and Brecht than Shakespeare'.[8] His interpretation is clearly influenced by Kott's reading of Shakespeare's *King Lear* and the theatre of Samuel Beckett.[9] *Waiting for Godot* and *Endgame* possess the same absurdist moments, the same explorations of nullity, the same examinations of the fragility of humankind as Shakespeare's *King Lear*, each being preoccupied with the 'nothingness' at the heart of human existence. In his film and in his 1962 RSC stage production, Brook transforms the play from Tragedy

[6] Christopher Sharrett, 'Introduction', in *Crisis Cinema: The Apocalyptic Idea in Postmodern Narrative Film*, edited by Christopher Sharrett (Washington DC: Maisonneuve Press, 1993), p. 5.

[7] Catherine Belsey, 'Shakespeare and Film: A Question of Perspective', in *Shakespeare on Film: Contemporary Critical Essays*, edited by Robert Shaughnessy (New York: St Martin's Press, 1998), p. 68.

[8] Normand Berlin, 'Peter Brook's Interpretation of *King Lear*: "Nothing Will Come of Nothing"', *Literature/Film Quarterly* 15 (1977),p. 300.

[9] Kott, p. 132.

to Grotesque, resulting in its cathartic and redemptive elements being underplayed and leaving us in a world devoid of consolation in line with Jan Kott's seminal critique of the text.

Michael Birkett, producer of *King Lear*, asserts their intention to avoid the kind of 'authenticity' that turns Shakespeare on screen into a museum piece. Instead, they create 'a setting dictated not by the nature of a particular moment in history, but by the nature of the play'.[10] Brook, wary of establishing a 'plausible world'[11] which may impede exploration of the text's complexities, creates a relatively blank canvas, peopled by characters whose stature and relationships are communicated by their performance and inter-action with the camera and its cuts, rather than by their costuming or use of elaborate props. Filmed in the frozen wastelands of Northern Jutland between January and April 1968, the locale of his *King Lear* remains purposely anonymous, devoid of cultural reference points and historical certainties. The production's non-committal costuming places the protagonists within a primordial setting but denies us anything more specific than that: Lear and his courtiers appear in sack cloth, Lear being singled out only by the enormous furs he wears in the opening moments of the film.

Brook is often criticised for failing to exploit the visual potential of film: he does deny us the standard visual shorthand provided by a loaded *mise-en-scène* – his sets are minimalistic and stark – and shots encompassing the epic grandeur of landscapes or castles symbolic of royal power form no part of his filmscape. But his choices are an integral part of his overall conception of the film,

[10] Roger Manvel quoting Michael Birkett in *Shakespeare and the Film*, p. 140.
[11] Brook quoted in Geoffrey Reeves, 'Finding Shakespeare on Film: An Interview with Peter Brook', first published in *The Tulane Drama Review* 11.1 (1966) in *Focus on Shakespeare Films*, edited by Charles W. Eckert (New Jersey: Prentice-Hall Inc., 1972), p. 38.

and he refuses to operate within the confines of the 'Shakespeare' or heritage genre, consciously denying what Jorgens terms the 'decorative spectacle'[12] audiences have come to associate with screen adaptations of Shakespeare, and rejecting the notion that Shakespeare's 'Elizabethan England' can be literally recreated on stage or screen. Instead, through the non-localised nature of his setting, Brook seeks to emulate the creative freedoms of the Elizabethan and Jacobean stage:

> I think that the freedom of the Elizabethan theatre is still only partially understood, people having got used to talking in clichés about the non-localized stage. What people do not fully realise is that the non-localized stage means that every single thing under the sun is possible, not only quick changes of location: a man can turn into twins, change sex, be his past, his present, his future, a comic version of himself and a tragic version of himself, and be none of them, all at the same time.[13]

Brook's counter-cinematic techniques, non-conventional editing and framing allow him to realise on screen both the multiplicity of Shakespeare's versification and the sense of fragmentation and inertia central to the image system he creates for his recon-figuration of *King Lear*. In so doing, he creates a film which highlights the process of storytelling whilst retaining the narrative momentum more readily associated with classical forms. The film plays with the classical design of *King Lear*, and Lear's conflict is internalised to a much greater extent in this treatment, whilst the rules of linear time and causality are unhinged by the use of silence,

[12] Jorgens, p. 245.
[13] Brook interview in Eckert, p. 38.

gaps in the narrative, and disjointed images created through experimental cinematography and editing techniques. In an interview conducted by Geoffrey Reeves in 1966, before production of his *King Lear*, Brook talks at great length about the relationship between play script and film as a medium, providing an invaluable insight into his role as an adapter of a Shakespearean text.[14] Shakespeare's verse is, according to Brook, redolent with surreal images and an anarchic potential which he exploits to the full in his screen adaptation. The shooting script contains numerous references to the increasingly surreal nature of the images, as they become 'less and less narrative, more and more strange, surrealist though never apparently fantastic'.[15] Kent's transformation scene at the start of Act One, Scene Four demonstrates Brook's capacity to use expressionistic cinematography to reflect the psyche of his characters. The on-screen images are fragmented through his use of jump cuts and a blurring of the focus, the camera zooming into and out of the image as if reflecting the pauses and shifts within Kent's mind in a style reminiscent of the stream-of-consciousness employed in prose writing.

One of Brook's major concerns revolves around what he sees as the 'consistency' of film images; they are too concrete to convey the multi-layered meanings of Shakespearean verse:

> The problem of filming Shakespeare is one of finding ways to shift gears, styles and conventions as lightly and deftly on screen as within the mental processes reflected by Elizabethan blank verse onto the screen of the mind.[16]

[14] Ibid., p. 38.

[15] Peter Brook, *Draft Shooting Script: King Lear* (9/9/68) reproduced by The Folger Library (Washington DC), Sc. 89.

[16] Brook in Eckert, p. 38.

In pursuit of this capacity to create on-screen images with the mobility and multiplicity of Shakespeare's verse, Brook toyed with the idea of creating a multi-screened projection, seeing it as 'a way that Shakespeare might be *found* on film'.[17] Employing techniques similar to those used by Abel Gance and the Cinerama would enable Brook to project the mental impression created by the verse:

> You see the actor as a man standing in the distance, and you also see his face, very close to you – perhaps his profile and the back of his head at the same time – and you also see the background ... you can have heath and the moment that a soliloquy begins you can drop the heath out of the picture and concentrate on different views of Gloucester. If you like, you can suddenly open a caption, write a line, write a subtitle. If you want, in the middle of a realistic action in colour you could have another or the same in black and white and the third captioned. You could have statistics or a cartoon parodying the photographic action.[18]

Today's cinema-going audience is far more film-literate and would not be surprised to find some of the devices Brook lists here employed in film. Movies as diverse as Oliver Stone's *Natural Born Killers* (1994), Quentin Tarantino's *Pulp Fiction* (1994) or Danny Boyle's *Trainspotting* (1996) make use of a variety of these counter-cinema techniques. However, in the early seventies, Brook was fully aware of the economic restraints upon his experimental talents, concluding that whilst he could employ some of these counter-cinema tech-

[17] Ibid., p. 41.
[18] Ibid., p. 38–41.

niques, the multi-screen concept would be 'economically hard to realise'.[19] He turned instead to directors like Godard and Antonioni for inspiration: Godard, he concludes, attacks the stability of the image or shot as a means of capturing its multiplicity whilst Antonioni accepts the stability of the shot but captures its invisible elements by employing a variety of devices. Both, most importantly, reject the notion that an individual frame carries meaning by and of itself. Brook's constant use of static shots embellished by other devices, such as creative editing and the suggestive power of what lies beyond the frame, is reminiscent of Antonioni's cinematic style. But he also employs the destabilising techniques characteristic of Godard's style in an attempt to create his desired sense of fragmentation, disorientation and alienation, the latter being a device 'of infinite possibilities … the only device which leads us back to the possibilities of blank verse'.[20] Brook has been criticised for his dominant use of static shots,[21] but such criticisms fail to take into account either the range and diversity of his cinematography or the rationale behind his cinematic style.

Given his apocalyptic interpretation of the text, Brook's image system must somehow convey a sense of fragmentation and sterility and this he achieves not only through the minimalist nature of the set and costuming, but through his cinematography and the ways in which he frames and edits the shots. The narrative transitivity of mainstream cinema, with its continuity editing and its explicit chain of causation, is rejected by Brook in favour of the kind of narrative intransitivity noted by critic Peter Wollen in the work of

[19] Ibid., p.41.

[20] Ibid.,p.40.

[21] Anthony Davies, *Filming Shakespeare's Plays: The Adaptations of Laurence Olivier, Orson Welles, Peter Brook, and Akira Kurosawa* (Cambridge: Cambridge University Press, 1988), p. 145.

Jean-Luc Godard.[22] Such an approach is engineered to distance spectators, constantly reminding them by interrupting the narrative, that what they are watching is a construct:

> Alienation is above all an appeal to the spectator to work for himself, so as to become more and more responsible for accepting what he sees only if it is convincing to him.[23]

Brook achieves this 'alienation' in numerous ways, by use of titles which tell us that we are, for example, at Goneril's castle or Gloucester's castle, or by interrupting the fluidity of the cinematography, employing canted shots and jump cuts which serve to disorientate the viewer, breaking the connection with the world of the narrative, as is the case in the opening moments of the film when we jump cut from Lear to Regan to Cordelia and back to Lear, as if in the blinking of the spectator's eye. His approach to editing is similarly conditioned by a desire to interrupt narrative flow: in a letter to Grigori Kozintsev, Brook states that in the editing process '(they) are searching to interrupt the consistency of style, so that the many-levelled contradictions of the play can appear'.[24]

He also frames shots in a way that suggests, at times, that we are standing behind characters, looking on from a distance rather than from an empathetic position, which again is characteristic of the counter-cinematic techniques noted by Wollen in the works of Godard, where 'estrangement' rather than 'cinematic identifi-

[22] Peter Wollen, 'Godard and Counter Cinema: Vent D'Est', *Afterimage* (Visual Studies Workshop) Autumn, 1972, pp. 7–16.

[23] Peter Brook, *The Empty Space* (London: Harmondsworth Penguin, 1972), p. 80.

[24] Grigori Kozintsev, *The Space of Tragedy: The Diary of a Film Director* (Berkeley: University of California Press, 1977), p. 241.

cation' is the desired effect.[25] When Lear responds to Cordelia's refusal to utter words of love with the line 'Nothing will come of nothing', (1.1, 90) we cut to a shot position directly behind Cordelia; we are denied access to her reaction and are forced to supplement this with our own. We have a clear focus on Cordelia in the foreground of the shot and yet it is the out of focus Lear who is speaking. Positioned as we are, we are distanced from Cordelia's reaction and yet experience a sensory identification with her as the viciousness of Lear's language reaches us. In this, Brook shares with Godard a desire to establish an interactive relationship with the audience, to engage with it at the level of intellect rather than emotion, and in so doing create a hero who is *less* tragic as an individual yet *more* so as a character representative of flawed humanity.

Whilst mainstream cinema requires us to identify with the protagonist, Brook's counter-cinematic approach aims for our estrangement and employs techniques such as direct address to camera, not as a means of giving us insight into the minds of characters, as is the function of the soliloquy in staged Shakespeare, but as a way of breaking the narrative surface to remind us that what we are watching is a construction of reality. Often, Brook's characters speak to camera when delivering lines of dialogue rather than soliloquies, forcing the audience into a discomforting viewing position and asking us to evaluate the truth of the spoken word as is the case when Lear's daughters are delivering, or withholding, their affirmations of love to him in the opening scene. Similarly, when Lear delivers his vile tirade against Goneril at the end of Act One, Scene Four, Paul Scofield delivers his lines direct to camera: the static nature of the extreme close up

[25] Wollen, p. 9.

shot emphasises the spoken word, forcing us to listen and to observe his performance (or delivery) in its finest detail. As viewers we are discomforted by his verbal onslaught, wanting to dissociate ourselves from his harsh language, but Brook demands our close engagement with the verse by the way he positions us in relation to the speaker. Russell Jackson notes that direct address to camera, when used to vocalise the soliloquy on screen, results in a 'radical disruption of the sense of the fictional space';[26] but Brook takes things a step further, using this kind of 'radical disruption' not only for delivery of soliloquies but for lines of crucial dialogue.

A tendency to emphasise the processes of production is also present. Brook's cinematography is extremely visible; the camera moves in a continuous arc from one face to another to deliver reaction shots rather than employing the swift, seamless continuity edits we are so accustomed to in mainstream cinema. For example, in the initial confrontation scene (1.4) between Lear and Goneril, the camera movements are highly visible: we circle Lear as his anger mounts, continually shifting our viewing position between Albany, Goneril and Lear via the moving camera rather than through continuity editing. Brook's use of hand-held camera creates a documentary feel to certain scenes and though contemporary cinema audiences may be de-sensitised to this kind of cinematography within narrative cinema, such a ploy was radical in the early seventies. As Lear exits in 1.2, denouncing Goneril and Regan as 'Hags', the camera jolts and moves around, lending the scene a sense of documentary-style immediacy and creating a feeling of unpredictability. The distorted framing and the camera move-

---

[26] Russell Jackson, 'From Play-script to Screenplay', in *The Cambridge Companion to Shakespeare on Film*, edited by Russell Jackson (Cambridge: Cambridge University Press, 2000), p. 25.

ment add to the fragmented image, infusing it with layers of instability and menace. Often there is also a level of incompatibility between the on-screen image and the accompanying sound: Lear's storm scenes contain a number of shots where the voice beyond the frame dominates and contradicts the stillness of the on-screen image. A total absence of music further underlines his desire firstly to deny conventional viewing expectations, and secondly to ensure that the word remains dominant. What Brook realises in his *King Lear* is a sense of radical instability operating at a filmic and an ideological level; unlike the 'safer' genre renditions of Lear's story, *his* film reflects successfully the innate sense of *textual* instability found in Shakespeare's play and in so doing creates a purposeful denial of assured interpretive positions in both texts.

Brook's desire to break away from the 'prison of photographic naturalism'[27] is evident from the opening moments of the first shooting script:

> On a blank screen, dots and blotches slowly materialise. What are they? Like an enlargement at the moment when the developer is just beginning to act, the disconnected patches are tantalisingly enigmatic. We try to link them, decide they make no sense, then suddenly from chaos a coherent shape emerges. A pair of eyes ... for a moment they are sharp and clear ... then they dissolve away again.[28]

Immediately, the opening images signal a disruption of the viewing experience. The focus upon the eyes emphasises the recurring motif

[27] Peter Brook in *Sight and Sound* interview (1965), quoted by Manvell in *Shakespeare and the Film*, p. 133.

[28] Brook, *Draft Shooting Script: King Lear* (9/9/68), Sc. 1.

of 'seeing', reminding us that we are participating in the act of intently watching something. The images cannot hold: they struggle to maintain reality – a comment, perhaps, on the nature of the medium and its incapacity to present the realism it aspires to. Further disjointed images 'fade in and die away ... define and destroy themselves',[29] reinforcing a lack of visual and narrative clarity in the opening moments. However, the final on-screen image bears no resemblance to these fragmented, disorientating establishing shots, despite their capacity to establish the over-riding sense of chaos at the core of Brook's interpretation. Instead, the establishing shots that make it to the screen strive to establish the feeling of inertia and of time suspended which permeates the whole film.

The film's opening moments illustrate the counter-cinematic approach adopted by Brook as a means not only of realising his apocalyptic vision of *King Lear* but also of creating an on-screen image redolent with multiple meanings of Shakespeare's verse. The establishing shot tells us little about the locale: in a nullifying silence and shooting in grainy black and white film stock, we pan a freeze-frame tableau of faces devoid of expression. An overwhelming sense of inertia is immediately established, the first panning shot lasting for thirty seconds before we cut to the title which reveals the title of the film and Shakespeare's name and capitalises on its cultural status. We then return to a reverse pan of the same frozen images, held for sixty-eight seconds, which seems endless. However, all faces now lean in one direction suggesting that something beyond the frame commands their gaze, and we too, as spectators, turn in anticipation, watching and waiting. Like Antonioni and Godard, Brook rejects the notion that an individual frame carries meaning by and of itself; by making his audience aware of the

[29] Ibid., Sc. 1.

significance of what is happening beyond the confines of the individual frame, Brook invests each frame with a multiplicity of meanings. The identity of the faces remains purposely ambiguous, though the second shooting script indicates that it is Lear's knights who are waiting outside, anxious about their predicament and conscious that great changes are imminent. As we edit to an interior shot the established sense of inertia continues to overwhelm the stark, shadowy set, dominated by a contradictory image of a tomb-like throne of phallic potency.

All things wait on Lear as we cut to a shot from the rear of his throne, the camera holding the moment once more for a further twenty-three seconds and building on the inertia established in the previous scene. We neither see nor hear from Lear during these moments of stillness; entombed in his coffin-like throne, his unconscious desire for death and annihilation is represented visually from the outset. However, the hierarchical positioning of others around his throne establishes a power structure with Lear at its apex and his importance is underlined by the way he continues to dominate film time. He is first presented in a static six second close-up shot, its low angle allowing him to dominate the frame as he says, `Know'. All superfluous dialogue is cut so that this isolated and negatively coded word becomes more potent. The shot is held for a further ten seconds, emphasising Lear's control of all things, even time it seems. The eerie stillness and the starkness of the scene add a disturbing edge to the proceedings, exacerbated by Scofield's monotonal, under-stated delivery. Even facial movement is minimal. The set is devoid of props, colour, depth of field, again adhering to Brook's desire to create visually the `nothingness' at the core of human existence, but also signalling to us the importance of the spoken word and performance. In the original shooting script we first see Lear `impatient' and `energetic', as he `climb(s) onto his throne',[30] but the on-screen representation gives us an inert Lear whose stillness and isolation lend dramatic weight to the opening. Brook's original intent was to frame Lear alongside a 'fussy and anxious'[31] Gloucester as Lear unrolled the map, but all changes at the production stage seem engineered to construct a more removed Lear, conscious of the way in which his position of power isolates him from all others, including his immediate family.

According to the shooting scripts, Brook's *mise-en-scène* was initially intended to be far more loaded and densely populated, giving a sense of the grandeur of the occasion and an outward display of Lear's wealth and status. In its final cut, there is no processional entrance and only a passing reference to the business of Cordelia's marriage to France or Burgundy. However, the first script speaks of one hundred knights, court secretaries, invited guests, whilst in the second script there is a much more detailed account of the room's décor, providing the kind of backdrop we would more readily expect of royal chambers and ceremonial gatherings:

> This is a small hexagonal chamber, almost a vault. Its walls are lined with bronze and let into them, in deep shelves, are the mummified remains of previous kings. At one end, the throne is backed and roofed in bronze, so that the king can sit inside it, like in an ancient studded chest.[32]

Brook's decision to film the ceremony using a much more minimalist approach allows him to realise that on-screen 'nothingness', which is an essential part of his image system, though the inclusion of 'the

[30] Brook, *Draft Shooting Script: King Lear* (9/9/68), Sc. 5.

[31] Ibid., Sc. 5.

[32] Ibid., Sc. 5.

mummified remains of previous kings' ranged on shelves would undoubtedly have added to Lear's presentation as a man already preoccupied with death. Lear's dialogue is also more extensive in both shooting scripts; by editing, Brook ensures our focus upon elements *he* perceives as being central to its thematic concerns. To begin, as intended in the script, with 'Give me the map' instead of 'Know' repositions the thematic focus from a concern with 'nothingness' to a preoccupation with the redistribution of power. By opening with the word 'Know', Lear's words are received as a command, an exercise not only of royal power but of fatherly power, the wisdom of which leads us to question the validity and the efficacy of the patriarchal power vested in him, exercised so randomly and without due care.

Apart from the throne, the coronet is the only prop weighted with iconic significance and it becomes a crucial emblem of Lear's royal power as he uses it to physically bestow the 'gift' of speech to his daughters. Given the overwhelming silence of the opening moments, we view the invitation to speak, and to legitimately break the silence Lear presides over, as an act of empowerment. Though the act of permitting speech is both controlled and administered *by* men, it is the women and their reaction *to* this gift that forms the dramatic focus of the scene in Brook's film, shifting the emphasis from Lear and, contrary to traditional readings of the text, inviting the spectator to view proceedings from the perspective of the daughters. Carol Chillington Rutter points out that it is during these opening moments of the play that Lear realigns the power-base by firstly authorising female speech and secondly appropriating female speech for himself in the guise of curses.[33]

[33] Carol Chillington Rutter, 'Eel Pie and Ugly Sisters', in *Lear: From Study to Stage*, edited by James Ogden and Arthur H. Scouten (London: Associated University Presses, 1997), p. 176.

Brook invests the ceremonious passing of the coronet and the ways in which it is handled by each of the daughters with a psychological subtext, communicated by his cinematography and his positioning of the camera's gaze. Goneril's lingering look at the coronet, which remains in shot, suggests that she is well aware of the power it represents, perhaps more so than Lear, and cannot quite believe he is ready either to relinquish all that it stands for or to legitimise her speech in this public arena. Goneril speaks to camera, positioning us with Lear and inviting us to judge the truth of her declarations of love for ourselves. Her delivery is measured, monotonal, well-rehearsed, and it is the first of many direct addresses to camera intended to disorientate the spectator and to disrupt our relationship with the fictional world.

Male control is still evident in these opening moments: the conch-like coronet is passed by Kent and Gloucester at Lear's bidding and Goneril, once she has delivered her speech, instantly seeks assurance from her husband that she has performed well. It seems that until licensed by Lear to speak she has been a far more compliant woman. However, from this point onwards Goneril's control of language increases in direct proportion to Lear's diminished powers of rhetoric. Lear, resorting to 'curses' as his only means of expressing his fury, further emasculates himself in the wake of female challenges to his power. During the course of the opening scenes Lear's language alters dramatically; the quiet commands of the patriarch, assured of his position and power, are displaced by the outraged curses of a man who has wilfully brought into question his own identity and sense of place within both familial and patriarchal systems.

Regan, in contrast to her sister, merely glances at the coronet. Her gaze is directed at Lear and her delivery is energised, sensual. Her desire to please Lear connects with us as spectators as she too delivers her lines direct to camera in a tightly framed shot. She says what Royal Lear wants to hear and the sexually charged nature of the delivery alerts us to the potentially incestuous undertones in her relationship with him – suspicions which are reinforced in Act Two, Scene Two when Lear threateningly flicks open the buttons on her bodice in a swift yet invasive act of male sexual aggression, engineered to intimidate. The sexually charged undertones are all the more successfully conveyed due to our positioning, her words seeming to be for us alone, despite the very public nature of the moment.

The way in which Brook edits to the isolated Cordelia is immediately suggestive of fracture and difference. The jump cut places her out of sync with her sisters and she is positioned in an almost painterly manner, sitting in the centre of the frame, the high walls towering above her, surrounded on all sides by empty space, no visual sign of male allegiances. She appears at this moment to be an isolated, diminutive figure. However, an earlier momentary glance from Goneril to Cordelia, engineered to seek Cordelia's compliance, becomes redolent with meaning at this point; despite Cordelia's current isolation, we sense a shared experience, a shared knowledge amongst all three sisters in their dealings with their father, Goneril's desire to appease rather than stir his wrath forming the subtext here. The veracity of the declarations of love delivered by Goneril and Regan have not been countered by any loaded asides from Cordelia in this film; Brook has purposely omitted such asides, constructing a picture of sisters who have shared in some unnamed and unutterable abuse. We do not read events in the tradition of earlier theatrical productions in which Goneril and Regan are demonised from the outset, whilst Cordelia stands as the epitome of virtue wronged.

Instead, Lear is presented as an overbearingly dominant patriarch with few redeeming qualities and any journeying towards redemption is undermined by the discomforting inference that Lear has in some manner abused his daughters. Paul Scofield does not present us with a frail, petulant old king but with a strong, aggressive ruler who is enraged by the notion that he will no longer be obeyed in all things, and whilst he does learn about the injustices of his world during the course of his journey, he moves not towards his own redemption but towards inevitable annihilation. Lear's daughters are given a much more complex representation – the demon/angel dichotomy is extinguished by the radical cutting of Cordelia's asides in Act One, Scene One, giving us less reason to doubt the veracity of the declarations of love given by Goneril and Regan, and adding credibility to the private conversation in which they voice their concerns about Lear's dubious dependability at the close of the scene.

When Cordelia steps up to receive the coronet she moves reluctantly into the static frame, gaze averted, refusing to connect with either Lear or the coronet; it weighs heavy in her hands, showing but momentarily before it moves out of shot completely, and signalling her lack of concern for all that it stands for. Cordelia seems unwilling to enter into a game she senses is controlled by men and their patriarchal systems. Unlike her sisters, she is not seduced by the promise of power and is wary of taking up Lear's gift of speech.

At the moment of confrontation the shooting scripts indicate their mutual intransigence: 'two refusals, two extremes', Cordelia displaying a 'Lear-like will', Lear a 'Cordelia-like refusal for compromise'.[34] When Lear commands her to speak, the static camera holds a close up shot of Cordelia for four seconds, suggesting through the silence the strength of her resistance. Lear's ensuing

[34] Brook, *Draft Shooting Script: King Lear* (9/9/68), Sc. 6.

verbal attack upon Cordelia is heard off-camera but we hold on a static close up of her, focusing upon the ferocity of his language. Critics may argue that by omitting her asides, Brook constructs a Cordelia who emerges as a petulant child unworthy of our sympathies, and whose banishment is deserved.[35] However, such assumptions fail to take into account the ways in which Brook engineers audience empathy both for Cordelia and her sisters: his point is that, in the initial stages at least, all three of them are more 'sinned against than sinning' (3.2: 60). Tellingly, Brook cuts from Cordelia to a menacing close up of Lear's angry face on his delivery of the phrase 'disclaim all my paternal care', (1.1: 114) visually demonstrating his rage at a moment when he is speaking of the 'paternal care' he ought to be exercising. Cordelia thrusts back the gift of discourse, symbolised by the coronet which remains the focal point of the frame, inferring that the giving of the gift is in itself a negation of paternal care.

Lear's inertia ceases at this moment: he emerges, bear-like from the depths of his throne, the chaos of this moment in which Lear's power is challenged being reflected in the initially chaotic camera movements. However, it is Cordelia's challenge to Lear's power that continues to dominate the scene. As France steps up to claim Cordelia her gaze remains averted and she is framed in profile in the foreground of the shot, the focus blurred: she is the object of male discussion but she has no power to influence proceedings as is indicated by her lack of clarity within the frame. When Lear moves into the background of the shot, his focus clear, his voice dominating, Cordelia remains in profile and out of focus; but as Lear delivers the lines 'nor shall ever see/That face of hers again' (1.1: 265–266), Cordelia slowly turns to confront him, seizing control

[35] Berlin, p. 301.

of the moment by turning her gaze upon him and, providing a visual contradiction to his discourse, she forces him to turn away from the power of her gaze. It is a direct challenge to Lear's power and it is asserted in silence, without recourse to the gift of speech he has tried to use to manipulate his daughters. Moreover, it is a turning point for female reappropriation of power, achieved without male license, through the silences more readily associated with woman's conventional position.

Its power to emasculate Lear is far more long-reaching than that afforded by the permitted speech of Goneril and Regan which serves merely as a cipher for the power of their husbands. Lear goes against cultural expectation when he condones female speech and in so doing he wilfully engineers his own downfall. At some unconscious level he desires death and annihilation, and it is this self-inflicted abdication not only of control but of language itself that propels him to the 'nothingness' that consumes him in the blank screen at the close of the film. When writing of the 'monstrous feminine' of the Horror genre, Barbara Creed argues that 'male castration fear is aligned with a masochistic desire for death'.[36] If we apply a similar logic to Lear's fear of being emasculated by his 'monstrous' daughters, his actions may be read as a masochistic wish-fulfilment of his desire for death: he instigates his own 'castration' and actively deconstructs his own identity. However, it is Cordelia's act of self-assertion at the close of the opening moments that signals the ultimate demise of patriarchal control and thus the death not only of Lear but of the patriarchal systems he perpetuates. Cordelia's Medusa-like gaze silences Lear and commands the screen space, ejecting him from the room.

[36] Barbara Creed, *The Monstrous Feminine: Film, Feminism, Psychoanalysis* (London: Routledge, 1993), p. 155.

As Lear exits we are reminded of the faces beyond the frame, watching and waiting upon Lear's every word, and it is to these faces that Lear now turns for reassurance of his power and identity. Yet the camera does not follow Lear's exit; instead it is Goneril and Regan who are given the final words in the act's moment of closure as we cut to their departure. The last words are given to the private female voice which requires no permission from Lear, and given the omission of all asides which suggest that Regan and Goneril will treat him badly, the concerns they voice seem well-founded and rational, especially when contrasted with the rash actions and ferocious language of their father. There remains a distinct lack of male heroism in Brook's film: Lear's descent into insanity is presented not as a journey of self-realisation and redemption but as a self-destructive pursuit of the oblivion he attains in the final frame. And although Brook constructs a strong voice for Cordelia in Act One, and an increasingly assertive voice for her sisters as the narrative progresses, their final demise is no more heroic than that of Lear.

On the road: reclaiming Grigori Kozintsev's Korol Lir (1970)

Whilst, historically, Kozintsev's *Korol Lir* has fallen into the category of canonised Shakespeare on screen it should, instead, be regarded as a genre product: it shares many of the structural, stylistic, thematic and ideological characteristics of the road movie, and has much more in common with the ambivalent road movies of the late sixties than with other screen versions of Shakespeare's plays of the time. It is a film which has been appropriated by Western academia as a 'classic' rendition of *King Lear* and is thus, one assumes, considered to belong to 'high culture' rather than 'popular culture' but as a writer/director operating within the parameters of Soviet Social Realist Cinema, Kozintsev's work was *destined* for a wider, more populist audience. A genre-conscious reading of *Korol Lir* demonstrates ways in which this film text has much more in common with genre cinema and with the socialist ideologies which underpin Soviet cinema of this period than with the kind of art house status conferred upon it as a result of its acceptance into the canon.

Korol Lir is the final film from Kozintsev's extensive filmography. His adaptation consciously moves away from the heritage screen versions of Shakespeare's works favoured by numerous directors at the time of the film's production,[37] but his treatment still offers a traditional rendition of the *Lear* tale, presenting us with definitive frameworks of good and evil, and a tragic hero who learns to correct his tragic flaw as the familiar, redemptive narrative unfolds. It conforms to expectations of accepted film practice and presents a *Lear* that is accessible to a mainstream audience, even in its subtitled format. Like other literary screen adaptations undertaken by Kozintsev in his final years,[38] it is devoid of the experimental elements embodied in his pioneering work as a member of the Soviet Montage School of film-making. By the late sixties, Kozintsev had become part of the Soviet film making establishment; there are few traces of Kozintsev, the experimental pioneer of the Soviet Montage School of film-makers in *Korol Lir*, and by this stage in his career his films no longer served as agents of social change. However, his adaptation of *King Lear* presents us with a sociological take on the narrative, drawing not only upon the Marxist ideologies that have always informed his thinking, but reflecting the socialist leanings of Russia at that time. *Korol Lir* emerged from the long-

---

[37] *The Taming of the Shrew* (1966), Franco Zeffirelli; *Romeo and Juliet* (1968), Franco Zeffirelli; *A Midsummer Night's Dream* (1968), Peter Hall; *Hamlet* (1969), Tony Richardson; *Julius Caesar* (1970), Stuart Burge; *Macbeth* (1971), Roman Polanski.

[38] *Don Kikhot* (1957), *Gamlet* (1963).

established state-sponsored production company Lenfilm and was one of twenty-one feature-length films created from 1969–70. The film industry thrived, despite residual state intervention, and unlike such contemporaries as Andrei Tarkovsky, Aleksandr Alov and Alexander Naumov who attracted state censorship in this era, Kozintsev toed the party line offering an array of 'heroic' images of the proletariat in his redemptive version of *King Lear*. His very Russian understanding of Shakespeare's play foregrounds the kind of 'Revolutionary Romanticism' noted by politics professor Richard Taylor as part of the Communist utopia.[39]

Kozintsev's treatment of the Shakespearean text as more 'tragic poem'[40] than play is reflected in his meticulous attention to the translation of its verse into cinematic images, yet it is the journeying motif, so central to Kozintsev's image system, that shifts his film from the provenance of art house cinema into the comforting realms of the universal and the generic. Whilst Kozintsev's depiction of the ordinary 'arithmetic of life'[41] helps to make the film a success, it is its predictable patterning, its striking thematic and ideological parallels with the mainstream road movie and its road movie iconography – whether employed at a conscious or sub-conscious level – that makes it an accessible, well-executed piece of genre film-making, tenuously and somewhat self-servingly labelled as art house cinema by academia.

Kozintsev's *Korol Lir* remains a tragedy but at an ideological and a thematic level it is also a fine example of the road movie genre characterised by its ideological stability and its dependence upon

---

[39] Richard Taylor, *BFI Companion to Eastern European and Russian Cinema* (London: BFI 2000). p. 218.

[40] Ronald Hayman, 'An Interview with director Grigori Kozintsev' in Eckert, p. 11.

[41] Kozintsev, *King Lear, the Space of Tragedy: The Diary of a Film Director*, p. 37.

a highly conventionalised value system. Dramatic conflict within this genre revolves around the protagonist's struggle to align – or realign – his views with those of the community at large, rather than upon the kind of territorial conflicts which shape narrative momentum in adaptations favouring gangster or western genre readings of Shakespeare's play.[42] Lear's journey of redemption, purposely excised from the latter type of adaptation, is central to the Shakespearean text and translates to the ideological template of the road movie with ease: territorial matters may provide the play's narrative momentum but it is the psychological turmoil Lear faces as he strives for his own redemption that forms its ideological core *and* that of Kozintsev's adaptation. His adaptations of Shakespeare's tragedies for the screen benefit from his in-depth understanding of their complexities as evidenced in his publications, *Shakespeare: Time and Conscience*[43] and *King Lear: The Space of Tragedy.*[44] He is, according to Ronald Hayman, 'one of the few directors with a deep feeling for literature';[45] unlike his contemporary, Peter Brook, Kozintsev's cinematic interpretation of *King Lear* is informed by Christian redemptive readings of the text in vogue in academic circles up until the late sixties.

And yet, despite his seemingly high-brow literary profile, it is Kozintsev's capacity to identify his Lear with the Everyman figure within this narrative that makes his film adaptation so remarkable. His Lear is 'a great king, the dominant personality in his kingdom. But he is also quite ordinary', and it is when Lear 'becomes like

---

[42] *House of Strangers* (1949); *Broken Lance* (1954); *The Godfather Trilogy* (1972, 1974, 1990), *My Kingdom* (2001).

[43] Grigori Kozintsev, *Shakespeare: Time and Conscience* (London: Dobson, 1967).

[44] Kozintsev, *King Lear, the Space of Tragedy: The Diary of a Film Director.*

[45] Hayman, p. 10.

everyone else' that 'his greatness as a tragic figure' begins.[46] It is not, in Kozintsev's hands, a film about heroic grandeur – his casting of the diminutive, softly spoken Yuri Jarvet as Lear speaks volumes here – and it does not follow traditional expectations of tragedy: our perception of the tragic hero is redefined, and it is 'the suffering of the whole universe', of 'the whole population of the country' that interests Kozintsev.[47] Furthermore, in highlighting Lear's redemptive journeying towards a better understanding of his subjects and himself, Kozintsev's ideological emphasis aligns itself with those of the genre of integration in which, according to Schatz 'conflicts derive not from a struggle over control of an environment but rather from the struggle of the principal characters to bring their own views in line with that of the larger community'.[48] We sense the presence of Kozintsev's peasants watching and waiting from the edges of the cinematic frame throughout the film as Lear's journey towards communal acceptance propels the narrative onwards; similarly Cordelia, seen here as the physical embodiment of the value system Lear initially chooses to reject, is seen to be constantly waiting out of shot for his return to the fold.

Korol Lir's affinity with the road movie genre extends beyond the ideological, its visual style echoing many facets of former and contemporary road movies popular at the time. The film is shot in 70mm Sovscope, a Russian version of the wide screen format associated with the road movie genre, giving an on-screen image which is twice as wide and twice as tall as standard film stock. Kozintsev's choice here is conditioned by his desire to move away from a depiction of Lear within the insular walls of his castles,

---

46 Hayman quoting Kozintsev, p. 11.

47 Hayman quoting Kozintsev, pp. 11–12.

48 Schatz, in Braudy and Cohen, p. 698.

placing him outside the fortifications, amongst his people; but it is also due to his desire to realise Shakespeare's text 'not only as a dialogue but as a landscape'.[49] Nature is given a specific role, 'like the chorus of a Greek tragedy',[50] and the landscape is frequently featured within the frame, suggesting its brooding presence at the core of the narrative as is often the case in road movies, whether such landscape is operating as the kind of malign force found in John Ford and Nunnally Johnson's film adaptation of *The Grapes of Wrath* (1940) or as a more ambivalent force in a film like *Easy Rider* (1969). The landscape itself is a polluted expanse of terrain near Narva, spoiled by the State Regional Electric Power Station. It is devoid of life and indicative of state destruction past and present, but it is also a landscape teeming with humanity and it is this that Kozintsev is at pains to highlight in the film's establishing shots. The collective experience is going to be of major importance within this Russian rendition of *King Lear*; the film's opening static frame is held for what seems like an unbearable length of time as Shostakovich's score adds a haunting edge to the confusing, claustrophobic image, an image which is barely recognisable as the woven fabric worn by the peasants who will soon dominate the screen, suggesting that it is they who will provide the canvas on which the tale is told.

However, this is the only point at which we sense inertia and it offers a stark contrast to both the sequence of shots that follow and the film as a whole. The all-important establishing shots, accounting for about five minutes of dialogue-free screen time, focus upon the landscape as Lear's people journey on foot or by makeshift transportation over this barren though densely populated terrain,

[49] Kozintsev, *King Lear, the Space of Tragedy: The Diary of a Film Director*, p. 26.
[50] Ibid., p. 26.

emphasising for us the significance of journeying in the film. These opening moments establish the iconography it shares with road movies of the period with its lingering shots of landscape, roads and means of transport. As we witness Lear's subjects journeying along the road to his castle for this royal occasion, the recurring shot of shuffling rag-bound feet traversing the rudimentary highway underlines the sense of perpetual motion which characterises Kozintsev's treatment of the text. Echoes of Ford's award-winning road movie take on Steinbeck's *The Grapes of Wrath* (1940), in which the Joad family represent the dispossessed in microcosm as they and their fellow workers traverse the dustbowls of a Depression-ravaged America, resonate throughout Kozintsev's *Korol Lir*. We move from shots of shuffling feet to the cart that carries a child, to horses ridden by soldiers, and as the narrative unfolds the camera continues to focus on images of people in motion, the method of transport, whether foot or horse, carriage or bier, being placed centrally within the frame. The repetitive nature of the shots here creates a kind of 'visual alliteration'[51] reminiscent of the overlapping editorial techniques employed by the Soviet Montage School in the 1920s and used to elongate the passage of time. The sequence culminates in a very painterly wide-angle shot held for four seconds: Lear's subjects frame its edges as they clamber over every vacant inch of hillside to strain towards Lear's castle, centrally placed to highlight its symbolic importance yet distanced in the background of the shot and shrouded in fog, as if less substantial than either the human beings who surround it or the land on which it rests. We return to such sequences throughout the film, bearing witness to the ways in which Lear's actions impact upon the masses, forcing them back on the road as exiles in a war-torn

[51] Ibid., p. 121.

country. The camera is continually drawn back to the landscape and the populace, underlining not only the film's affiliation with the road movie genre in terms of its subject matter and its cinematic style, but with the socialist ideologies underpinning Kozintsev's reading of the *Lear* text.

It also shares with road movies a recurring use of wide-angle shots of open vistas with roads stretching on beyond the edges of the frame in a style reminiscent of road movies of the period from *Bonnie and Clyde* (1967) to *Butch Cassidy and the Sundance Kid* (1969), to *Easy Rider* (1969). Kozintsev continues to engineer landscape scenes in which we witness the perpetual motion of Lear and his subjects. We see Lear and his entourage as they journey relentlessly from castle to castle; we view Cordelia's journey into exile; Edgar's wanderings with itinerant beggars; Gloucester and the mad Lear meandering through the wilderness. These patterns of perpetual motion, again bearing acute similarity to Ford's *The Grapes of Wrath*, provide the 'visual generalisations' which for Kozintsev 'grow into a movement', giving 'shape and dimension' to the sequence of the shots,[52] inferring once more that the journeying motif which dominates the road movie genre is central to his image system. Similarly, the on-screen marriage of Cordelia and France 'not in a church, but on the road'[53] signifies the iconic importance of the road and the journeying motif within this film. Furthermore, there is a predominance of the wide-angle tracking shots characteristic of the road movie as Lear moves from castle to castle and as his people gather not only in the opening moments but as bands of wandering exiles forced into motion by the onslaught of a civil war during the course of the film. Speaking at UNESCO HQ in Paris

---

[52] Ibid., p. 35.

[53] Hayman quoting Kozintsev, p. 12.

in 1964, Kozintsev claimed that the essence of film adaptation is to develop aspects of the play which are not as accessible to the stage.[54] By employing the visual signifiers and cinematic style associated with the road movie genre, whether at a conscious or a subconscious level, Kozintsev has been able to realise a version of *King Lear* which it would be impossible to create in the theatre given his stress upon landscape and journeying at both a literal and metaphorical level.

Once we move into the confines of the castle walls, Kozintsev again loads the scenes with a sense of relentless motion and employs a heavily loaded *mise en scène*. Only at this point do we move to the opening dialogue of the source text which is built around Boris Pasternak's translation of the play. We see Gloucester and Kent walking as they discuss Lear's decision to divide his land; we see courtiers lining the walls and servants coming into and going out of shot, taking up positions for this important occasion; we witness the arrival of Burgundy and France as they assume their positions, flanked by their entourage and by their royal insignia. It is a scene peopled by a shifting population all of whom are there at Lear's bidding, as are his subjects beyond the walls of the castle. Kozintsev constructs an orderly and very public space, 'as similar as possible to contemporary diplomatic receptions: polite, inscrutable faces: the savage animal hidden behind a civilized exterior',[55] working in direct contrast to the visual disorder presented by the peasants beyond the walls of the court. This seemingly civilised space, punctuated by public rituals, is yet another sign of conformity to the expectations of the genre of integration; but Kozintsev plays with expectation here since the value system of the

---

[54] Manvell, p. 80.

[55] Kozintsev, *King Lear, the Space of Tragedy: The Diary of a Film Director*, p. 42–43.

court is exposed as corrupt: the 'civilised space' is to be found instead beyond the confines of the castle walls.

The heavy-handed stereo-typing of Goneril and Regan is instantly conveyed; in everything from their costumes to their movement, they stand in visual opposition to the virtuous Cordelia, and Kozintsev denies them their closing moment at the end of Scene One, purposely editing out their doubts as to Lear's reliability and undermining any sense that they are operating together out of necessity from the outset. The moment is instead given over to close up images of a vulnerable Lear presided over by his 'evil' daughters. They are the 'savage animal hidden behind a civilized exterior'[56] to which Kozintsev continually alludes through use of symbolic editing, reminiscent of the Soviet Montage School of film-making, cutting from shots of Goneril and Regan to close up shots of dogs, chained and salivating as the narrative progresses.

Conversely, Cordelia transcends the stereo-typical and is synonymous with virtue, the 'fair warrior' whose act of rebellion is a consequence of her naturalness[57] rather than her perversity. She is introduced in motion as she hurriedly descends the stairs, seemingly oblivious to court etiquette; her difference is emphasised visually not only by the stark contrast of her simple white attire and its blatant associations with innocence and virtue but by the clarity of her image, framed in a warm, bright light at all times. However, the visual allusion to Carl Dreyer's *Jeanne d'Arc* (1928) is quite striking, investing her with strength and a warrior-like dimension that belies her vulnerability from the outset. With the exception of these opening scenes, she is continually framed within shots dominated by the natural world beyond the castle walls. Like Kozintsev's

56 Ibid., p. 42–43.
57 Ibid., p. 70.

peasants she is aligned with nature and water imagery throughout. She becomes the film's physical embodiment of rebirth and renewal, symbolic of its redemptive possibilities, particularly in her closing moments. The final image of the hanged Cordelia is set against a backdrop of free-flowing water; we then cut to a frame in which her corpse is erased from the shot, leaving us with the dominant image of the running water that, in keeping with Kozintsev's redemptive reading of the Shakespearean text, speaks of hope and regeneration.

Given the attentive nature of the court as it awaits Lear's arrival, we anticipate the entrance of some grand monarch of epic proportions but Kozintsev undercuts expectation, heralding Lear's arrival by the off-screen sounds of laughter and jingling bells which jar with the solemnity of the now static interior shot. Our first glimpse of Lear reveals a diminutive, white-haired old man, barely distinguishable from the Fool with whom he shares this frame. Their relationship from the outset reflects certain aspects of the camaraderie that is so often a convention of the road movie genre; just as Butch has his Sundance, Lear has his Fool, though the 'buddy' elements of this narrative are often overshadowed by the text's darker undertones. Lear assumes a domestic pose, warming his hands at the hearth (an image associated at an iconic level with notions of family and home), and fondly stroking his Fool's head, their behaviour clashing with the serious intent of the waiting courtiers. Again, Kozintsev's image system is constantly dependent upon the kind of symbolic juxtaposition readily associated with the Soviet Montage School of film-making, and this is one aspect of his later work which clearly connects with his earlier cinematic style, as Lear's association with nurturing images of fire and domesticity are displaced. At a rather simplistic level, whilst Cordelia and Kozintsev's peasantry are synonymous with the purifying elements of water and nature, King Lear (and the court he presides over) is aligned with fire imagery that infers volatility and destruction.

In the closing moments of the opening sequence we alternate between shots of Cordelia's leave-taking and Lear's hurried departure, the tranquillity and simplicity of the former contrasting with the mayhem and huge scale of the latter. Lear's train is associated with images of brutality: we see the Fool dragged along on a chain and we cut once more to low-angle shots of dogs and birds of prey. From here, Lear ascends the outer staircase, his figure diminished by the scale of the architecture, his isolaton from the rest of humanity highlighted as we cut initially to the waiting crowds in a high-angle shot which momentarily magnifies their powerless-ness but that swiftly switches to a high-angle shot of the isolated Lear, cloaked in the fog of the symbolic flames burning upon the parapets. As Shostakovich's dramatic score builds in momentum, we are presented with an image of Cordelia and France positioned on the brow of the hill, as if watching over Lear from a distance, establishing a sense of their continued presence, the final frame of the opening sequence holding on a low-angle shot of the misty horizon and returning us to the notion that, as in all road movies, the landscape is a brooding presence in and of itself.

Kozintsev's stress upon the redemptive nature of the *Lear* story and upon Lear's journey of self-discovery places it, in one sense, alongside earlier road movie narratives as diverse as *The Wizard of Oz* (1939) and *The Grapes of Wrath* (1940), both of which deal with similarly redemptive journeys of self-discovery, the road 'function(ing) as an alternative space where isolation from the mainstream permits various transformative experiences'.[58] The

---

[58] Steven Cohan and Ina Rae Hark, 'Introduction', in *The Road Movie Book*, edited by Steven Cohan and Ina Rae (London: Routledge, 1997), p. 5.

protagonists in all three films set out on a path of reconciliation of some kind, ultimately attained by both physical and spiritual journeying and all the protagonists internalise their conflict, albeit in the guise of Dorothy's dreamscape in *The Wizard of Oz*. Dorothy's often nightmarish dreamscape, in which she seeks to break free from family constraints, ultimately leads her to what is packaged 'Hollywood-style' as a universal truth – 'There's no place like home' – whilst Kozintsev's Lear journeys into the depths of insanity and despair in order to rediscover a similar sense of well-being afforded by his return to the ideological and, in this instance, decidedly Marxist-Christian fold. However, Lear's journey is, like that of protagonists in other road movies of this time, 'cowled in lurking menace, spontaneous mayhem and dead-end fatalism'.[59] The preoccupation with 'home' is an obsession of the genre: 'home' functions as 'a structuring absence'[60] and whilst Dorothy learns to value the home she was so eager to leave behind, Kozintsev's Lear has a much more ambivalent relationship with familial structures. Timothy Corrigan argues that the road movie is a genre that not only 'responds to the breakdown of the family unit' but 'witnesses the destabilization of male subjectivity and masculine empowerment';[61] the breakdown of such patriarchal institutions as 'family' forms part of the ideological fabric of both Shakespeare's play and Kozintsev's film text, Lear's preoccupation with his mistreatment at the hands of his offspring functioning as a 'structuring absence' during his journey and leading him to the borders of insanity as his identity is

[59] Michael Atkinson, 'Crossing the Frontiers', *Sight & Sound 1* (1994), pp. 14–18.

[60] Pamela Robertson, 'Home and Away: Friends of Dorothy on the Road in Oz', in *The Road Movie Book*, eds. Steven Cohan and Ina Rae Hark (London: Routledge, 1997), p. 271.

[61] Timothy Corrigan quoted in 'Introduction', in *The Road Movie Book*, edited by Steven Cohan and Ina Rae Hark, pp.2–3.

'destabilised' in response to the self-willed disintegration of his role as patriarch of both family and kingdom. This 'unhinged masculinity' is, according to Aitken and Lukinbeal, part of the 'hysteria' brought about by road movies 'precisely because hegemonic concepts of masculinity seem to become unhinged'[62] as we move beyond the 'safe' confines of family and patriarchal institutions. In *Korol Lir*, concepts of masculinity are 'unhinged' by Lear's daughters, Goneril and Regan, but he remains unable to move on, his concept of himself being 'embedded within the logic of patriarchy'.[63]

The structural parallels between *Korol Lir* and its road movie forerunners in terms of the shared *desire* for final reintegration is central to the thematic patterning of the road movie genre. The climactic point in Kozintsev's *Lir* does not revolve around the deaths which are so central to the drama in the genre of tragedy; instead, it is Lear's reconciliation with Cordelia that provides the climax, focusing our attention at a thematic level upon the importance of redemption and a return to the fold, even if only temporarily given that their deaths follow swiftly on from this moment. We move from what Schatz terms the position of 'romantic antagonism' central to the genre of integration to its predictable final 'embrace', signalling Lear's *spiritual* reintegration in classic road movie style. However, Kozintsev's Lear welcomes the opportunity to withdraw to the confines of a prison cell rather than envisage reintegration into the politically debased society he once ruled and death is the preferred option once Cordelia, the embodiment of 'civilised' society, is violently removed. The contemporaneous *Butch Cassidy*

---

[62] Stuart Aitken and Christopher Lee Lukinbeal, 'Disassociated Masculinities and Geographies of the Road', in *The Road Movie Book*, edited by. Steven Cohan and Ina Rae Hark, p. 366.

[63] Ibid., pp. 366–367.

and the Sundance Kid presents us with a similarly violent close to that of *Korol Lir*, 'buddies' Butch and Sundance, like Kozintsev's Lear, choosing death rather than reintegration into the civilised society they have been at odds with, and discovering in the process their own form of freedom or 'romantic embrace'.[64]

Whilst Hollywood films of the forties like *The Wizard of Oz* and *The Grapes of Wrath* follow the formulaic route meticulously, with all issues neatly resolved by the end of the journey and the prescribed Hollywood closure in place, *Korol Lir* shares with road movies of the sixties and seventies certain twists, moving away from conclusive endings and unproblematic reintegration into the communal fold. Despite their seemingly cosy propensities, road movies can be read as 'songs of the doomed';[65] films like Arthur Penn's *Bonnie and Clyde* and Denis Hopper's *Easy Rider* form part of a progressive yet brief period in American cinematic history when film-making became artistically ambitious, and these films' violent, apocalyptic, non-Hollywood closures share striking similarities with Kozintsev's *Korol Lir*, the final emphasis being upon death, futility, emotional bankruptcy. Like the protagonists of standard Hollywood road movies such as *Sullivan's Travels* (1941), Lear has 'travelled through danger and disillusionment to healthy self-knowledge and back to the safety of home',[66] but his successful reintegration into *dominant*

[64] Just as Butch Cassidy has his Sundance Kid, Lear has his Fool whose role is extended in *Korol Lir* (both physically and thematically) beyond that which he has in the source text. He also becomes, in many readings of the play, a pseudo-Cordelia – a physical embodiment of her absence.

[65] Atkinson, pp. 14–18.

[66] Thomas Waugh, 'The Third Body: Patterns in the Construction of the Subject in Gay Male Narrative Film', in *Queer Looks: Perspectives on Lesbian and Gay Film and Video*, edited by Martha Gever, John Greyson, and Praibha Parmar (New York: Routledge, 1993), p. 143.

culture remains an impossibility. Regardless of Lear's redemption and his reintegration into the Marxist-Christian fold, epitomised by Cordelia and the peasants who remain a waiting force on the edges of the cinematic frame, the film's final moments have more in common with the apocalyptic images of late sixties Crisis Cinema than with the kind of neat reintegration into mainstream society expected of the pre-sixties road movies.

Korol Lir follows the narrative pattern established in Shakespeare's play, but here the subtext is generated by Kozintsev's socialist leanings: Lear rejects his former position of power, aligning himself instead with the values epitomised by a Cordelia who is synonymous with the proletariat beyond the castle walls. Kozintsev does offer closure of some kind but it remains a tentative ending, leading us to ponder the apocalyptic potential of our future. We are invited to believe, as with Edward Bond's *Lear*, that life is ultimately full of redemptive possibilities: the integral use of water imagery symbolic of rebirth and renewal ensures this as do the closing moments of the film in which the stoic peasants douse the flames of war. However, Kozintsev allows his audience the opportunity to interpret the close in a number of ways, dependent upon the viewer's reading of the final shot of Edgar. Edgar's closing lines are cut and he looks directly into camera, reminding us of the illusory nature of his film world and momentarily forcing us to engage with the bigger questions the narrative has posed via this direct address to the watcher.

We are left to make our own assumptions as to whether Edgar is likely to restore order and if so whether he – or indeed anyone – can prove to be a virtuous ruler operating within an autocratic system. The stress upon the importance of the collective community is yet another predictable pattern within the genre of integration to which the road movie belongs, and it is significant that Kozintsev ensures our continued awareness of the presence of Lear's 'collective community', not only in the opening and the closing moments of his film, but in the inclusion of the cinema audience in the final frame as Edgar invites us to engage in the debate through his direct gaze into the camera's lens. *Korol Lir* may be offering a redemptive, uplifting message in one sense, but we cannot escape the violent, apocalyptic elements embedded in either the source text or, through its intertextual allusions, the apocalyptic road movies prevalent in Western cinema at the time of the film's production.

Kozintsev employs a conventional approach to the narration of a well-known and often-told tale. Although he avoids the trappings of the heritage genre so readily associated with adaptations of Shakespeare to screen, his film conforms to mainstream expectations in many ways: from its adherence to classical narrative forms, to its use of accepted film practice, its construction of clearly delineated archetypes to its associations with the stylistic, thematic and ideological properties of the road movie genre. In adopting the stylistic and ideological motifs of this genre – a genre which shares with Shakespeare's *King Lear* a place within the 'longer tradition of the journey in literature and myth'[67] – Kozintsev produces a film text that reflects the apocalyptic propensities of the original and connects with the 'songs of the doomed' sung in the road movies of the late sixties, the journeying motif lending itself to the kind of visual representation possible only within the realms of cinema. Despite its appropriation as canonical screened Shakespeare by Western academia, Kozintsev's *Korol Lir* should be

[67] Michael Hammond, 'The Road Movie', in *Contemporary American Cinema*, edited by Michael Hammond and Linda Ruth Williams (Berkshire: Open University Press, 2006), p. 15.

reclaimed as a film that has much more in common with populist cinematic genre forms than with auteur-driven art house cinema.

Chaos on the Western frontier: Akira Kurosawa's Ran *(1985)*

Kurosawa's film successfully melds the literature of East and West, the film genres of the jidai-geki epic (*see* p. 83) and the mainstream western, and the cultural/stylistic motifs of Japanese cinema and theatre with the codes and conventions of Hollywood. Yet despite its Eastern affiliations, *Ran* has remained the property of decades of Western scholarship, acclaimed as part of a *Shakespearean* heritage of global proportions. Western academics persist in the assertion that it is first and foremost a version of a Shakespeare play, some seeing it as a paradoxical contradiction that Kurosawa would deny it is a direct adaptation of *King Lear*.[68] The film is not afforded autonomy regardless of its independent aesthetic value; rather, it remains, in the eyes of Western film and Shakespeare criticism, dependent upon the 'original', and is thus trapped by a discourse of adaptation that valorises what is seen as its Shakespearean source text.[69] There is little discussion of its intertextual strengths and no consideration of the film as a highly successful work of genre cinema.

Kurosawa claims that, despite the many narrative and thematic connections between his film and *King Lear*, its initial sources come from Japanese histories, mythologies and theatrical practices rather than from Shakespeare's play text:

[68] Ann Thompson, 'Kurosawa's *Ran*: Reception and Interpretation', *East–West Film Journal* 3:2 (1989), pp. 1–13.

[69] Mitsuhiro Yoshimoto, *Kurosawa, Film Studies and Japanese Cinema* (Durham NC: Duke University Press, 2000), p. 260.

I had the idea about writing something about the sixteenth-century Japanese war lord Mori Motonari, who had three sons. And having written an outline of the script, it suddenly occurred to me that it was very similar to *King Lear*, so I went back to read it again, and developed it from there. Motonari had three very good sons, so I started thinking about what would have happened if they hadn't been loyal, and developed a fiction around the actual character.[70]

Written in collaboration with Hideo Oguni and Masato Ide, the screenplay and resulting film are based largely on a desire to invert the Montonari legend. In Kurosawa's adaptation, Motonari, powerful ruler of the Ichimonji clan during the Sengoku era, decides to relinquish control of his empire to his three sons, Taro, Jiro and Saburo. Though dutiful and loyal according to legend, in Kurosawa's telling of the tale, these sons become synonymous with Lear's daughters: Taro and Jiro feign obedience whilst the youngest son, Saburo, who questions the wisdom of his father's actions and is exiled as a consequence, emerges as Motonari's only loyal offspring. Kurosawa's fictionalised version of the legend also gives prominence to the wives of the eldest sons. The families of both wives have been ruthlessly defeated by Motonari and aligned with the Ichimonji clan through marriage, but each wife's response to her family's demise is strikingly different. Jiro's wife, Sué, epitomises forgiveness, but Taro's wife, Kaede, is motivated by revenge, and it is her revenge quest that supplements narrative momentum in this adaptation. It is her manipulation of Taro and Jiro that leads to Motonari's ultimate demise and to that of the Ichimonji clan.

[70] Akira Kurosawa quoted in Anne Billson, 'The Emperor', review, *Time Out*, 12 March, 1986, p. 14.

Credited with bringing Western critical acclaim to Japanese cinema and an affirmation of its status as a national cinema, Kurosawa has found himself criticised for attracting Western enthusiasm. Despite his proclaimed commitment to Japanese culture, he is often regarded by Japanese critics as a film-maker overly concerned with creating images which are accessible to a Western eye rather than being true to their Eastern origins. As a result of some disastrous box-office failures in the seventies, Kurosawa's ventures in the eighties were dependent upon overseas funding. Francis Ford Coppola and George Lucas provided American financial backing for his film *Kagemusha* (1980), whilst *Ran* was dependent upon Serge Silberman's French funding.

However, regardless of its dependency on foreign funding, *Ran* is a distinctly Japanese film product. In his approach to the film, Kurosawa consciously adopts the theatrical conventions of Noh theatre which provide not only a structural framework for his narrative by establishing the `patterns of polarity and disparity'[71] associated with this form, but also a stylistic template which embodies the form's aesthetic ideal of `simplicity-as-complexity'.[72] The dichotomies which operate at the root of Noh theatre are employed at a visual level, leading to the construction of images of abstract simplicity, and frames infused with an astonishing sense of symmetry. *Ran* is a film that is striking in a visual sense, so much so that reviewers have often been critical of the film as a consequence, seeing Kurosawa's attention to the visual beauty and sophistication of the on-screen image as a detraction from its potential psychological energy. Peter Ackroyd, writing for *The Spectator*,

[71] Keiko McDonald, *Japanese Classical Theatre in Films* (London: Associated University Presses, 1994), p. 142.
[72] Ibid., p. 125.

claims that *Ran* is 'Shakespeare drained of its poetry, stripped of its human dimensions, and forced within a schematic framework derived from quite different attitudes and preoccupations'.[73]

The influence of historical theatrical practices upon Kurosawa's directorial style is in evidence throughout *Ran*. However, whilst his work imbibes elements of the benshi tradition,[74] potentially posing a very different viewing experience for Eastern and Western audiences, Kurosawa's films retain a populist Western appeal that challenges their definition as art house cinema. His painterly style is a by-product of Japanese cultural influences as opposed to a sign of his anti-genre leanings. *Ran*'s narrative deals in archetypal characters and follows a classical story design rather than the non-linear narrative patterning and psychological preoccupations associated with art house films; and despite the highly stylised, artistic nature of its images, its deployment of visual, structural and ideological motifs readily associated with the western genre ensures its accessibility to a global mainstream audience. More-over, unlike Western adapters, Kurosawa can use ideas and images from *King Lear* without being hindered by concerns for the 'sanctity' of Shakespeare's verse,[75] leaving him free to realise the essence of the Shakespearean text and the Eastern narratives it engages with in other, much more cinematically visual ways. By exploring the spatial dimensions of the screen image dialogue

[73] Peter Ackroyd, '*Ran*', review, *The Spectator*, 15 March, 1986, p. 37.

[74] John Collick, *Shakespeare, Cinema and Society* (Manchester: Manchester University Press, 1989), p. 169. Collick claims that, due to the benshi's influence on the evolution of Japanese cinema, the Japanese film-maker and his Japanese audience is, historically, trained to 'read' film as a collection of symbolic images rather than as a medium which should be passively viewed as a reality.

[75] Anthony Davies, *Filming Shakespeare's Plays: The Adaptations of Olivier, Welles, Brook and Kurosawa* (Cambridge: Cambridge University Press, 1990), p. 23.

becomes almost redundant; his dependence upon visual and aural signifiers, as opposed to verbal signifiers, is in part realised by his use of Noh theatrical conventions and the spatial dimensions associated with that dramatic form.

Although operating within the realms of a distinctly Japanese costume drama, unlike heritage reworkings of Shakespeare's plays, *Ran* does not become merely an exercise in visual excess. By employing the jidai-geki genre, which is associated with glorification of the samurai and its very masculine code, Kurosawa proceeds to illuminate not only the flaws within the code but the redundancy of its 'heroes', disrupting viewing expectations of Western and Eastern audiences. Set in a culturally and historically specific sixteenth-century feudal Japan, during an era known as the Sengoku Jidai and peopled by samurai warriors and war lords, it plays with the conventions of jidai-geki, subverting audience expectations by challenging the conventional notions of heroism and loyalty associated with the very Japanese values of the samurai. Yet despite working through a Japanese aesthetic, Kurosawa's global acceptance is in part due to his capacity to imbibe elements of Western film practice, especially in relation to his samurai epics. His earlier samurai film, *Shichinin no Samurai* (1954), pre-empts many of the thematic concerns explored in his later samurai films, including *Kumonosu Jo* (1957), *Yojimbo* (1961), *Kagemusha* (1980) and *Ran*: all embody Kurosawa's pre-occupation with the transience of the samurai warrior and the codes and conventions by which he lives, and most explore the samurai's relationship with the land. His archetypal 'heroes' – like the heroes of Shakespeare's tragedies – remain far more problematic and complex than their generic Hollywood counterparts.

Contrary to Western perceptions of samurai honour and obligation, betrayal was an intrinsic part of feudal Japan, the master-servant relationship being far from stable, and the extermination of a lord by one of his own ambitious samurai not uncommon.[76] The flawed myth of samurai honour and might, perpetuated by the jidai-geki genre, is exposed in *Ran*: there are no *effective*, mythical heroes. The reincarnation of elements of *King Lear* as a western, whether in frontier USA[77] or feudal Japan, demonstrates the narrative's capacity to be used as raw material employed in the exploration of the 'myths' of other nations, within the context of other historical eras. Like Kurosawa's samurai epics, *Ran* is indebted to the westerns of John Ford: Hidetora displays an affinity with Ford's lone heroes, placed within monumental landscapes characterised by territorial conflict. However, in *Ran* Kurosawa creates a film text which deconstructs the myth of the samurai and that of similar frontier myths of the lone hero explored in Hollywood's western genre.

Genre-based adaptations of *King Lear* have traditionally presented us with an essentially male-centred quest, revolving around the Everyman figure of Lear and operating within a macho, male-dominated society. Numerous screen versions employ the *Lear* narrative, albeit loosely, within what film academic Thomas Schatz refers to as the genre framework of 'order' or 'determinate space', a genre 'type' characterised by its 'ideologically contested space(s)'. The all important setting becomes what Schatz terms ' the cultural realm in which fundamental values are in a state of sustained conflict'.[78] The western's classification as a genre of determinate space predetermines the story's thematic concerns and its ideological position, leading us to expect a certain type of macho hero operating within a clearly defined cinematic world.

---

[76] Collick, p. 152.

[77] See *Broken Lance* (1954).

[78] Schatz in Braudy and Cohen, pp. 696–698.

We anticipate the ideologically contested setting in which society's values remain in flux, conflicts over territory and value systems providing the narrative momentum. Ostensibly, the western's story arc moves towards an eventual ordering of the chaos as frontier values are imposed and the 'wilderness' is 'tamed', but its turning points revolve around violent conflict and the innate instability of these frontier lands remains a constant, even when adhering to the neat, formulaic closures of the Hollywood studio system.

If we view Kurosawa's *Ran* as a pseudo-western it too can be classified as belonging to the genre of order in a structural, an ideological and a thematic sense. Social disintegration and the violence inherent in such breakdown remains at the core of both *King Lear* and the western genre, their heroes and those of Kurosawa's feudal Japan sharing an ambivalence towards the values of civilised society. Edward Dmytryk's western, *Broken Lance*, presents a reconfiguration of the Lear myth in which the territorial conflicts are seemingly resolved in true Hollywood style by the close of the film. Like Hidetora, lone hero Matt Devereaux has been instrumental in ordering the initial chaos and finds his hard line values no longer work within the kind of 'civilised' society that now emerges. However, Devereaux's demise is a consequence of progress and follows the story line of the conventional western whereas Hidetora's demise is initially self-inflicted. Mirroring the actions of Shakespeare's Lear, Hidetora brings on the chaos by relinquishing control, subverting our expectations of the samurai lord and by inference the western hero whose function is to tame the wilderness rather than willingly surrender control of it.

As with the western, *Ran*'s sense of place is pivotal: its ideologically contested setting becomes of central importance, the rugged landscape forming a 'symbolic arena of action'[79] similar to

[79] Ibid., p. 696.

that of the western's frontier plains within which conflict persists in the absence of a stable milieu. The vast landscape is foregrounded by Kurosawa and its brooding presence becomes part of the film's fabric – a constant situated at the edges of the frame, seemingly 'tamed' by the might of the samurai warlord Hidetora Motonari yet threatening always to engulf humankind and its 'civilising' influence. Robert Warshow argues that the landscapes of the western serve to diminish, rather than magnify, the stature of the western hero.[80] In much the same way, the samurai is invariably pitted against a frontier-like landscape in Kurosawa's *Ran*, highlighting their fragility and that of their value system throughout the narrative. Through allusion to the topographical and iconographic signifiers of the western, Kurosawa creates a world in which questions of honour and loyalty are played out against a backdrop of epic proportions, and in which violence and conflict are the norm.

Hidetora is constructed as the archetypal western hero; he is, in Schatz's genre terminology, 'psychologically static', the 'physical embodiment of an attitude, a style, a world-view of a pre-determined and essentially unchanging cultural posture'.[81] Unlike Shakespeare's King Lear, Hidetora does not seek redemption and his 'heroic' deeds remain questionable, devoid of any motivation other than a lust for power; he is not 'a man more sinned against than sinning' (3.2: 59–60). We learn of his violence against the families of Sué and Kaede, and of his vicious treatment of the peasants who work the land he rules. He has little to say about self-discovery, with such speeches as 'Who is it that can tell me who I

---

[80] Robert Warshow, 'Movie Chronicle: The Westerner', in *Film Theory and Criticism*, 6th edition, edited by Leo Braudy and Martin Cohen (Oxford: Oxford University Press, 2004), p. 709.

[81] Schatz, p. 695.

am?' (1.4: 221) – speeches indicative of moments of inner-reflection – finding no place in Kurosawa's screenplay, and he retains the isolated, distanced stance of the western hero. There are glimpses of Hidetora's conscience and he does become more reflective as his power unravels; but when he asks Sué how she has found the capacity to forgive his violent actions, he is incapable of understanding her Buddhist beliefs and leaves with nothing, unable to feel after a lifetime of violent excess. His conflicts are externalised and we are given few insights into the psychological turmoil triggered by his abuse at the hands of his sons.

Such externalisation of conflict is again more reflective of the western genre of mainstream cinema than of the tragic conventions we associate with the Western stage. Indeed, Yoshiko Ueno claims that the whole concept of personal tragedy is alien to Japanese culture since 'the search for individual identity, which is usually assumed to be a major focus of *King Lear*, is alien to Japanese thought'.[82] In *Ran* there is no sense of the redemptive heroic sacrifice which we have come to associate with Western tragedy. Only Hidetora's wives and concubines are seen to perform the heroic act of sepuko when he is faced with defeat inside the burning castle walls. Kurosawa devotes considerable screen time to Hidetora's unsuccessful attempts to mirror their honourable act, visually subverting the conventional portrayal of the samurai hero. Those invested with a sense of the heroic die: Saburo and Sué are eliminated and we sense that the feuding will continue with Lords Fujimaki and Ayabe simply taking over from the Ichimonji clan. The samurai as a social community emerge as a decidedly unheroic collective, devoid of principled heroes. Both Taro and Jiro are constructed as self-serving males who allow

[82] Yoshiko Ueno quoted in Thompson, p. 8.

themselves to be manipulated by Kaede, and Kurogane's attempts to restore samurai honour by slaying the treacherous Kaede are undermined by our knowledge of his own dishonourable acts, not least his cowardly killing of an unsuspecting Taro.

The opening moments of the film illustrate the very tenuous nature of samurai power, positioning the warriors against the backdrop of a landscape which totally overwhelms them, dwarfing them within the frame. Despite the openness and fertility of the surrounding landscape, we sense the discomfort of those held within the frame; the four armed riders, meticulously positioned to enhance the symmetry of the shot as they look out to the four points of a compass, remain unnaturally still. Intrinsic sound is eliminated from what should be a very naturalistic moment and is replaced by a sound track reminiscent of the horror genre, its high-pitched strings jarring with the serenity of the landscape, enhancing the sense of discomfort experienced by the riders and the audience. In the series of shots that follows, Kurosawa's attention to the visual balance of each frame remains a stylistic feature: we see three different riders positioned in a line against the backdrop of the mountains, followed by a shot that encompasses five of the riders, again symmetrically placed in a hierarchical formation, again each holding a static pose, the gaze of all riders looking out in the same direction. At this point all sound is eliminated, adding to the tension within the scene and creating a feeling of unsettling inertia that clashes with our expectations of the macho figures held within the camera's gaze.

Even though their masculinity is signalled through costuming and their appearance in masculine pose on horseback, their stillness and anxiety are at odds with the preconceptions we hold of the samurai warrior or of their heroic western counterparts. They are constructed as an anonymous alien presence, impinging upon a landscape established in the opening moments as a brooding entity which will remain throughout the film. Kurosawa creates a tenuous symmetry within these opening shots, visually demonstrating the fragility of each frame's balance and in so doing infers a similarly fragile image of masculinity. The suggestion that each frame can be so easily disturbed – by a sound, by a movement – is analogous to his construction of masculinity; a masculinity that holds on to power by futile attempts to order the chaos through codes and conventions which, as in the frontier landscapes of the western, cannot be sustained without brute force. Through the very staged nature of the opening frames, reflective of the visual simplicity of Noh theatrical conventions, Kurosawa highlights the notion that man's attempts to order the chaos cannot succeed and, moreover, that masculinity is a construct which can easily be *de*constructed. The final image within the sequence leaves us with the kind of wide-angled panoramic landscape shot we have come to associate with the western. The human figures appear as miniscule, inconsequential blemishes on the canvas of the landscape, pre-empting the film's bleak closing sequence in which the masculine samurai warriors are replaced by the lone figure of the emasculated Tsurumaru who, though visibly their antithesis, shares with them a vulnerability signalled by the sheer dimensions of the natural world that overwhelms them.

It is against this iconic backdrop, reminiscent of the western plains, that we are given our first glimpse of Hidetora, the first of the figures seen on screen to be invested with any detailed representation. Rather than viewing the scene from the distanced stand-point of the establishing shots, we are brought down to the boar's eye level in a rare point of view shot, the boar centrally placed front of camera, positioning us as spectators with the hunted animal. From the powerless position of those who watch and wait, the warriors now emerge into the shot from below our sight-line, the embodiment of masculinity and physical aggression, subverting the expectations Kurosawa establishes in the opening frames in which they appear to be the hunted rather than the hunters, and yet again setting up parallels with what is to come later: the hunter Hidetora ultimately becomes the hunted despite his warrior-like stance as he first enters this sequence in dynamic hunting pose, commandeering the screen with his presence whilst the camera tracks his pursuit of the boar, and visually conveying his prowess through the magnificence of his costume and his unrivalled horsemanship, both of which set him apart from the other faceless warriors. He is clearly the most imposing hunter, held firmly in the camera's gaze as he draws back his bow to shoot the boar, and a swift edit to the film's title, *Ran*, further underlines his central role within the narrative, creating a visual shorthand that immediately associates him with the chaos and violent disorder that ensues.

However, in western film text – and in Shakespeare's play – there emerges what Barry Langford terms 'an almost contradictory inter-dependency of wilderness and civilisation'.[83] We move to a very staged scene in which we see war lord Hidetora imposing order on the vastness of the landscape that surrounds him; three tented areas are erected, the black and gold of Hidetora's insignia taking centre stage and providing limited shelter from the open, natural spaces that seem to engulf them. The attempted domestication of the landscape is strikingly at odds with the surroundings, and the fragility of the structures erected to signify Hidetora's control and place within the hierarchy of politics and family again lead us to

---

[83] Barry Langford, *Film Genre: Hollywood and Beyond* (Edinburgh: Edinburgh University Press, 2005), p. 65.

question the stability of each. We are not presented with an image of the war lord Hidetora framed by the might of the castles he has constructed or acquired during his reign, but by the flimsy canvas structures he has erected to mark out his territorial authority and dominance. The transitory nature of the image presents us with a visual realisation of the ambivalent relationship between the binary oppositions of 'wilderness' and 'civilisation' outlined by Kitses as essential to the ideological framework of the western genre.[84] Any sense of order remains transitory – a mere nod to the 'taming' of the 'wilderness'. Even when we cut to the more substantial images of Hidetora's castles, these man-made fortresses seem inconsequential when framed against the backdrop of the plains they are perched precariously upon. Placed on the borders of the unruly frontier Hidetora, like the archetypal western hero, becomes representative of both its lawlessness and its social order, initially able to 'mediate the forces of order and anarchy, yet somehow remaining separate from each',[85] and never completely secure in his power position within the 'contested spaces' of the film world he inhabits.

Hidetora's mask-like appearance and sumptuous costumes lend his figure a regal air; he is a powerful war lord rather than a doting father, much as King Lear is constructed firstly as a powerful monarch and secondly as a man who craves outward shows of affection from his children. But as with King Lear, his regal mask slips to reveal the vulnerable and needy old man; although seated at the apex of the power triangle staged within the confines of the tented arena he presides over, he dozes, presenting a direct contrast to the opening image of the hunter Hidetora and leading us to question the stability of the power constructs we are

[84] Jim Kitses, *Horizons West* (London: Thames and Hudson Ltd, 1969), p. 11.
[85] Schatz, p. 696.

presented with. Kurosawa's inverted re-enactment of the Motonari tale, in which he examines what would happen if Motonari's sons were to prove disloyal, provides a visual shorthand for the oncoming chaos that will form the narrative momentum of the film. Saburo quite rightly foresees the chaos and violent disorder that will not only consume the world of the samurai but also the tenuous loyalties at the heart of the Ichimonji family should Hidetora's control be relinquished. It is the warrior pose of Hidetora, established during our first glimpse of him, that must be maintained if the chaos of the title is to be contained. Kathy Howlett suggests that Hidetora feels trapped 'in a rigid system of samurai identity' from which he wants to escape, and cites his frantic desire to quit the tented enclosure he has created, after experiencing a nightmare vision of his own isolation within it, as proof of his subconscious intent.[86] But his 'tragedy' ensues when he tries to realise his desire to become other than the distanced hero upholding a certain code of ethics in a morally volatile world. Hidetora can only 'mediate the forces of order and anarchy'[87] which typify the contested spaces of both a feudal Japan and the unruly frontier when he maintains his position of relative separation.

Issues related to the disintegration of identity are explored via the concept of failed – or failing – patriarchy in *King Lear*, *Ran* and the western genre, and in each there remains an inescapable element of wish-fulfilment to the demise of the paternal figurehead. Signs of Hidetora's weakness and offered tendernesses in the opening sequences are rejected by Saburo since he sees Hidetora's identity as war lord and leader of the Ichimonji clan as

[86] Kathy Howlett, *Framing Shakespeare on Film* (Ohio: Ohio University Press, 2000), p. 121.

[87] Schatz, p. 696.

being of far more import than his desire to change his role to that of doting, dependent father – a role which has no place within the conventions of a feudal samurai Japan and one which, given Hidetora's past, he is destined to find almost impossible to sustain. By publicly relinquishing control Hidetora is relinquishing his masculinity, redefining his identity and thus amplifying the vulnerability of those who live by the samurai code: his actions ensure not only his own demise but that of the samurai. When Saburo states, 'We too are children of this age, reared on strife and chaos', he clarifies the position of the samurai warrior (and by inference the western genre's counterpart) who must battle to ensure order, to maintain the masculinity at the heart of the samurai code, or face its extinction. Even when 'playing' the role of benevolent father, through Kurosawa's distancing of the spectator and the continued absence of reaction shots, close ups and shot-reverse-shot sequences, Hidetora's emotional credibility remains circumspect, especially when coupled with a performance that is highly theatrical and stylised, and spatial positioning which highlights the formal nature of relationships.

This new identity constitutes a fragile framework, as vulnerable and exposed as the image of the riders who form part of the opening tableau. Despite the warrior-like pose held by Hidetora as he first enters the frame, there are subtle indications that his masculine image will be continually undermined during the course of the film; the subsequent recurring shots in which Hidetora is framed in doorways and through windows are more readily associated with the ways in which women are framed on film.[88]

[88] Carol Chillington Rutter, 'Looking at Shakespeare's Women on Film', in *The Cambridge Companion to Shakespeare on Film*, edited Russell Jackson (Cambridge: Cambridge University Press, 2000), pp. 242–243.

Within the formal tented enclosure, Kurosawa constructs an image of Hidetora as the majestic, tyrannical old man of Noh theatrical conventions, his face painted with the mask-like properties of the Akujo.[89] He is clearly the intended focus of our gaze, his masked appearance contrasting with the naturalism of the other faces within the frame and his opulent costuming overpowering the primary colours of his sons and the black and white costuming of Ayabe and Fujimaki. However, as with later shots of Hidetora in doorways and through windows, we see his face in this formal moment framed by his headgear, its symmetrical lines holding his face for the camera's gaze, again suggesting a shot composition more often employed when suspending an image of the female form, and thus adding to the deconstruction of his masculinity.

During the course of the narrative the only 'heroic' individual is eliminated: in a moment which is cinematically inconsequential, Saburo is unceremoniously shot as he rides with the rescued Hidetora, his death momentarily passing unmarked. Those who have adhered only to the violence of the samurai code have suffered a similar end, Taro, like Saburo, being shot not during the onslaught of battle but during a shockingly quiet moment. There are no heroic confrontations in which the might of the samurai is established; the only shot which sustains a heroic image of samurai warriors on horseback comes as Saburo's troops vacate the Third Castle, the blue and white plumes of the riders dominating the screen from a low-angle shot. Even so, they are seen leaving rather than holding their position. Saburo is physically aligned with the regenerative attributes of the natural world and is seen only within the open spaces of that natural world throughout the film; yet, despite his good intentions and his visual affinity with nature, he is

[89] McDonald, p. 141.

unable to sustain the role of masculine hero, suggesting that Kurosawa is again asking us to contemplate the inefficacy of masculinity and the patriarchal systems on which it is inherently dependent. It is the emasculated Kyoami who remains as protector of Hidetora during the course of the narrative, leading us to question the roles of sons and samurais.

Unlike the more conservative western genre adapters of fifties Hollywood, Kurosawa's intertextual referencing of the *Lear* story uses the concept of powerful, demonised womanhood. Female lead, Kaede, is neither the 'happy whore' nor the dependable, domesticated 'pioneer homemaker' of the conventional western genre, though there are warped elements of each within her on-screen persona. Despite her diminished position as a woman in a feudal Japan Kaede, in contrast to the men around her, emerges as a character able to retain her own codes of honour and family loyalty. She operates within the confines of her social position (as do the women of the western genre) as a seemingly powerless woman and yet she is the perpetrator of horrendous acts of violence which ultimately lead to her planned disintegration of the Ichimonji clan and the samurai code. Kaede embodies the histories of demonised woman in Japanese folklore and theatre;[90] but Kurosawa skilfully intertwines this with allusions to demonised womanhood at the core of Western mythologies via visual references to the serpent as iconic of woman as temptress in both cultures. Her persona is also invested with elements of the archetypal monster of the horror genre. Her seduction of Jiro plays with horror conventions: elements of the sexually predatory vampire are embodied in the seduction sequence as her 'penetrating mouth,' biting and licking blood,

[90] Zvilca Serper, 'Lady Kaede in Kurosawa's *Ran*: Verbal and Visual Characterisation Through Animal Traditions', *Japan Forum* 13:2 (2001), pp. 148–149.

becomes what horror critic Darryl Jones terms a 'displaced version of the familiar phobic image of the vagina dentata, simultaneously enveloping and castrating'.[91] Contrary to cinematic conventions, Jiro becomes the feminised focal point of the camera's gaze and Kaede becomes the epitome of Barbara Creed's 'monstrous-feminine'[92] challenging accepted notions of femininity which, by definition, equate with passivity. Like the big-hearted prostitute of the western genre she is a sexualised being, but there is nothing passive about Kaede's sexuality. Actively performing the role of castrator, Kaede usurps the male position, wielding Jiro's knife as part of her sado-masochistic foreplay and orchestrating the downfall of the Ichimonji clan through her manipulation of its supposedly 'heroic' samurai lords.

As the males around her demonstrate their weaknesses and their inability to uphold the values of the samurai code they supposedly live by, Kaede strives to undermine the conventions that are pivotal to that code and to matters relating to family honour and loyalty. Her own loyalty to family is proven, the role of daughter being far more important to her than that of dutiful and submissive wife, whereas the sons of Hidetora, the next generation of the Ichimonji clan, have shown themselves to be either disloyal and dishonourable or ineffectual and unable to wield patriarchal control. However, by challenging gender traits, Kaede, like Goneril and Regan in Shakespeare's *King Lear*, ensures her own reconstruction as demon. Kurogane's decapitation of Kaede serves as a re-assertion of patriarchal dominance, her figure finally framed and contained by the legs of the males who surround her. Inevitably, she is executed

[91] Darryl Jones, *Horror: A Thematic History in Fiction and Film* (London: Arnold, 2002), pp. 85–86.

[92] Creed, p. 152.

because she is a threat to samurai values and the samurai identity, linked as it is to the masculinity she has sought to destabilise.

The heroic stature of warlord Hidetora is undermined continually as he, like the archetypal heroes of mainstream westerns, tries to renegotiate his position within this unstable world; having maintained control through his violent, despotic leadership, he is unable to see that to relinquish his control will unleash anarchy. The film's ideologically contested space, in which territorial conflicts are an historical given, becomes a site of violent social disintegration on a par with the societal disintegration found in westerns in general and *King Lear* in particular. In Kurosawa's realisation of a feudal Japan the values of the samurai are in flux: the landscape may have been tamed by Motonari and a social order established, but his capacity to hold back the wilderness which threatens to engulf his world at any moment is limited, and forms the narrative momentum of the film. Despite Kurosawa's reputation for creating what are regarded as very masculine films, in *Ran* it is this disintegration of masculinity and patriarchal institutions which provides the narrative focus, and it is in this respect that Kurosawa's film connects with Shakespeare's *King Lear*, the dramatic exploration of the demise of patriarchy underpinning each text's ideological and thematic preoccupations. Furthermore, Kurosawa draws parallels between his potentially anarchic feudal setting and the western frontier, and in so doing deconstructs the cult of masculinity at the core of both genres. In the absence of firmly established frontier or samurai codes of conduct alike, the precarious stability such codes help to maintain dissipates and the cult of masculinity which underpins them disintegrates.

Kurosawa's depiction of patriarchy in crisis leads to an apocalyptic close in which all suffer and none are redeemed, and we are led to the conclusion that the very masculine codes and values at the core of patriarchy are destructive, inherently violent and unsustainable: *this* apocalyptic vision is devoid of the redemptive heroism we more readily associate with Shakespeare's play. *Ran* and *King Lear* proclaim their preoccupation with universal truths and a scepticism of the validity of patriarchal institutions at both a familial and a political level. However, whilst Kurosawa's depiction of the demise of patriarchy shares with its Shakespearean counterpart a concern with those who transgress gender boundaries, it is the dilution of the masculinity at the core of samurai values which sets *Ran* apart and ensures that it remains a work invested with its own 'cultural capital', existing within its own cultural reference points, Shakespeare's decidedly Westernised version of the play operating here as intertext rather than source text. Although widely regarded as part of the canon of Shakespeare on screen and appropriated by a Shakespearean heritage of global proportions, Kurosawa's *Ran* refuses to be consumed by its Western affiliations and asserts instead its affiliations with the western genre in terms of its ideological premise and its iconic properties. If, as Tony Howard suggests, the conventions of the western can be seen as a reinstatement of Renaissance codes of conduct revolving around issues of masculinity and 'poetic justice',[93] then the codes and conventions of the samurai may also be viewed as such. However, what Kurosawa dramatises in *Ran* is the demise of the samurai, and by inference the demise of the western hero and Shakespeare's tragic hero, deconstructing the heroic myths of masculinity which surround these iconic figures in literature and film on a global scale. His film offers a social critique of patriarchal systems across a range of genres, from

[93] Tony Howard, 'Shakespeare's Cinematic Offshoots', in *The Cambridge Companion to Shakespeare on Film*, edited by Russell Jackson (Cambridge: Cambridge University Press, 2000), p. 299.

Japanese jidai-geki epic to Renaissance tragedy, to Hollywood western, linking the concerns embedded in Shakespeare's *King Lear* with those of other historical eras, other nations, other mythologies.

King Lear and genre cinema

King Lear has been reconfigured as mainstream genre cinema in various guises for over fifty years. In some genre readings of the text, the narrative has remained closely linked to Shakespeare's play. Intransigent, domineering father figures at the head of various empires replace Shakespeare's similarly all-powerful Lear, and daughters are sometimes replaced by sons as the forces that bring about his downfall. In *House of Strangers* (1949), *Broken Lance* (1954), and *My Kingdom* (2001) the narratives track the demise of father-figures Gino Monetti, Matt Devereaux and Sandeman who, though undermined by outside governmental forces, are ultimately betrayed from within. The downfall of empire is written into the script of Shakespeare's play and each of these genre films. Whilst all three patriarchs retain the love of a good Cordelia-like son/daughter, they forfeit the love of their other offspring as a result of their own incapacity to behave fairly towards them. Just as Monetti's banking empire collapses and is rebuilt by his wronged sons, Devereaux's ranching empire is saved through the sacrifice of his son, Joe, only to fall into the hands of Joe's antagonistic half brothers. Similarly, in *My Kingdom* control of the mobster family empire passes from Sandeman to his *Lear*-like evil daughters, Kath and Tracey, and the film's Cordelia figure, Jo, divorces herself from the family and its mobster mentality as the Sandeman family's grip on Liverpool's mafia underworld disintegrates.

The relationship between Coppola's *Godfather* gangster trilogy and *King Lear* is more tenuous and presents a far less literal reading of the text. Instead it appropriates certain elements of the story: its ideological concerns, its familial betrayals, and its protagonist's ultimate desire to extricate himself from the burdens of leadership permeate all three *Godfather* films to varying degrees, each film building towards the more overt parallels shared between the *Lear* text and *Godfather III*. The films may not follow the narrative trajectory of Shakespeare's *King Lear* to the extent of the previously mentioned genre films, but there are fascinating points of reference between the man Don Michael Corleone eventually becomes and the hero of Shakespeare's tragedy.

Operating within the very different realm of women's melo-drama, *A Thousand Acres* is a screen adaptation of Jane Smiley's revisionist version of the *Lear* story in which the tale is told from the perspective of his abused daughters. Smiley's epic cast of characters remain closely connected to their Shakespearean counterparts and her story-line mirrors that of Shakespeare's play in most respects, though it explores Ginny's journey of recognition and redemption rather than that of her abusive father, Larry.

Each adaptation is considered here in relation to both Shakespeare's *King Lear* and the genre framework it employs: the relationship between the ideological preoccupations of genre and the play text is examined in close detail, as are their respective archetypal and narrative templates, their iconographic and stylistic modes of expression.

King Lear *as western elegy: Edward Dmytryk's* Broken Lance *(1954)*

The western's central position in the history of American cinema is well documented. It is a genre which has attracted considerable academic debate despite rather than because of its mainstream appeal and its association with the studio system. From the era of silent cinema to its demise in the seventies, the western reigned supreme with around one hundred westerns being produced and released a year at the peak of its popularity in the fifties.[94] Measured against the backdrop of westerns made in the early fifties – *Broken Arrow* (1950); *Devil's Doorway* (1951); *High Noon* (1952); *Shane* (1953) – and preceding marginally John Ford's *The Searchers* (1955), Edward Dmytryk's *Broken Lance* builds upon the kind of social criticisms being explored in these westerns, offering a commentary on the hypocrisy, racism and opportunism at the core of a post-war America in the guise of the historically removed frontier western. Dmytryk's film is often cited as a reworking of Shakespeare's *King Lear*, hero Matt Devereaux's sons being the cinematic equivalent of Lear's daughters, and there is some scholarly debate about the similarities between Shakespeare's play and this film text. However, with the exception of Tony Howard's very brief critique of *Broken Lance*[95] and Robert F. Willson Junior's blow-by-blow account of connections between characters in play text and film text,[96] there is little academic discussion of this adaptation, even though it is a film which poses interesting parallels with the *Lear* narrative at a thematic and an ideological level.

This film's protagonist, like Shakespeare's Lear, relinquishes control of his lands. However, it is as a consequence of his own violent law-breaking that self-made cattle rancher Matt Devereaux is forced to hand over his property to his sons for safe-keeping. It is an act of self-preservation taken under duress rather than a wilful relinquishment of power of the kind Lear precipitates at the start of Shakespeare's play. Devereaux's sons (three, from his first

---

[94] Langford, p. 57.

[95] Howard, in *The Cambridge Companion to Shakespeare on Film*, pp. 295–313.

[96] Robert F. Willson Jr., *Shakespeare in Hollywood: 1929–1956* (New Jersey: Associated University Presses, 2000), pp. 115–122.

marriage), with the exception of his youngest (mixed race offspring, Joe, whose 'exile' takes the form of a prison sentence in reparation for his father's lawless acts), prove untrustworthy, and the film's narrative plots his descent as his empire crumbles around him.

In westerns like *Broken Lance* the 'symbolic arena of action' is all important as the setting becomes what Schatz terms 'the cultural realm in which fundamental values are in a state of sustained conflict'.[97] We anticipate a certain type of macho hero operating within a clearly defined cinematic world, where conflicts over territory and value systems provide the narrative momentum. *Broken Lance* does follow the familiar western formula but it is also a veiled exposé of American society, its inherent prejudices and racism. In addition to its Golden Globe award the film won a best writer's Oscar for Philip Yordan. This western and his earlier screen adaptation, *House of Strangers*, are both loosely based on Jerome Weidman's novel *I'll Never Go There Anymore* – a novel which in turn borrows from Shakespeare's reconfigured narration of the *Lear* myth. Moving the text to the frontier landscapes of America may seem a radical shift from the thematic and ideological premise of Shakespeare's play but, as Tony Howard suggests, western conventions mirror Renaissance codes of 'masculinity and poetic justice'; the proud 'founding fathers' of the frontier become the American equivalent of a patriarchal Lear whilst daughters become sons, reflecting the sexual conservatism of fifties Hollywood.[98]

Social disintegration and the violence inherent in such breakdown remains at the core of both *King Lear* and the western genre. Their heroes share an ambivalence towards the values of civilised society and as such it is hardly surprising to find that the *Lear* myth

---

[97] Schatz, in Braudy and Cohen, pp. 697–698.
[98] Howard, pp. 297–298.

has been used on occasion by Hollywood as a narrative template for the western genre, and most recently as televised western *King of Texas* (2002). In *Broken Lance* the ideologically contested space, in which territorial conflicts are an historical given, becomes a site of violent social disintegration. Devereaux's fierce defence of his land leads to the unlawful lynching of cattle thieves and the anarchic destruction of the Associated Western Copper and Refining Company's mining operation which is polluting his water supply and killing his cattle: however, his violent responses to any infringement upon his hard-earned territorial gains – responses which once ensured his capacity to tame the frontier wilderness he functions within – set in motion the disintegration of his empire. The codes by which frontier heroes like Devereaux live are being superseded by those of an emerging 'civilisation'. The old order with which Devereaux aligns himself is associated with the land, dictatorial authority and a macho sensibility; in much the same way, certain readings of *King Lear* present us with a proactive autocratic monarch who is the agent of his own downfall, rather than an elderly victim of society's neglect seeking the redemptive path. Devereaux's ideological position as archetypal western hero is undermined by the emergence of a new order motivated by self interest, bourgeois values and a 'civilised', institutionalised *modus operandi*, whilst Lear's position as ruler, once relinquished by his own act of division of his territories, is swiftly and irredeemably usurped by a similar new order motivated by self interest and epitomised by Edmund, Goneril, Regan, Cornwall and Oswald. Lear's claim that he will 'resume the shape' that Goneril believes he has 'cast off for ever' (1.4: 301–302) rings hollow, as does Devereaux's empty threat to have the state governor he claims to have 'put in that chair' removed unless he appoints a judge who will find in his favour in the prosecution brought against him by the copper mining company. Both texts explore the transitory nature of power and the fragile value systems underpinning them.

The play's reincarnation as a western demonstrates its capacity to be used as raw material employed in the exploration of other 'myths' at the forefront of society's consciousness. Ostensibly a male-centred quest played out against a backdrop of contested territory, the western's sense of place is pivotal: the 'frontier' becomes its 'conceptual axis',[99] transforming historical material – in this instance US frontier country of the 1890s – into 'archetypal myth'.[100] The western constructs a genre framework of mythical proportions comparable to that achieved by Shakespearean tragedy; however, unlike Shakespeare's *King Lear*, the western is, by its very nature, contained by its historical context. It is a genre of exteriors in which the landscape is constantly foregrounded; *Broken Lance*, shot in wide screen Cinemascope, opens with a conventional panning shot of the wide open plains, establishing its genre status through a *mise en scène* loaded with western iconographies and accompanied by a traditionally dramatic orchestral score. We move to the anticipated shots of the developing western frontier town, where the government building, the bank and the Foothill Land Office epitomise its progression from make-shift frontier settlement to 'civilised' town, providing in visual shorthand a sketch of the film-world's contested spaces – the wilderness of the plains pitted against the evolving civilisation of the town, the archetypal western hero at odds with the institutions of government in accordance with the binary oppositions identified by Kitses as central to the ideological preoccupations of the western.[101]

[99] Langford, p. 62.
[100] Ibid., p. 62.
[101] Kitses, p. 11.

Devereaux's association with the open plains which dominate the opening and closing frames of the film underline the importance of his relationship with the land, his image becoming intertwined with that of the lone wolf who traverses the landscape in each scene. Although *King Lear* is a text which is free from chronological and geographical constraints, it shares a parallel preoccupation with the land from the outset; mapping the division of the kingdom – its contested spaces – forms the focal point of the opening moments, the map (and the territories it defines) symbolising Lear's power and his affiliation with the land. What is staged through the ceremonious division of the land at the start of the play is presented cinematically in *Broken Lance* via the lingering shots of the frontier landscape that will be contested throughout the narrative.

However, in western film text – and in Shakespeare's text – there emerges what Barry Langford terms 'an almost contradictory interdependency of wilderness and civilisation'.[102] Placed on the borders of the unruly frontier, the western hero becomes representative of both its lawlessness and its social order, initially able to 'mediate the forces of order and anarchy, yet somehow remaining separate from each'.[103] Devereaux tames the savage landscape and establishes a kind of social order: he is a solitary figure who yet remains the agent of a civilisation that ultimately resists his individualism and his ambivalent attitude towards the values of that emerging society. Devereaux's portrait continues to dominate the grand foyer of Government House even after his demise, demonstrating his continuing significance to the fragile civilisation he has worked to establish but which has inevitably

---

[102] Langford, p. 65.
[103] Schatz, p. 696.

rejected his brand of law and order – a law and order which is generated by his own codes of honour and integrity, and which are at odds with the increasingly institutionalised, community-minded civilisation being cultivated as part of the newly tamed frontier.

As archetypal western hero, Devereaux's screen persona is confined by the generic expectations of the fifties Hollywood studio system, leading to a much more black and white exploration of the solitary hero than we have come to expect of the protagonist in staged productions of *King Lear*. The hero's complexities and his inner turmoil are excised in *Broken Lance* in pursuit of genre clarity, Devereaux's frustrations being presented cinematically by his outward shows of physical and verbal violence rather than through any exploration of his psyche. Like Kurosawa's Hidetora, he is, according to Schatz's genre terminology, 'psychologically static', the 'physical embodiment of an attitude, a style, a world view of a predetermined and essentially unchanging cultural posture'.[104] The film also follows Hollywood conventions in its desire to give clarity via the inclusion of back-story that justifies Devereaux's lack of paternal care for his sons from his first marriage; whilst we are left to ponder the ambiguities of Lear's actions we are provided with a rationale for Devereaux's behaviour. In response to Señora Devereaux's claim that he has 'never given them anything of (himself)', Devereaux argues that he had no time to show his motherless sons love because he was busy building up his ranching empire. Lear's lack of emotional sensitivity is similarly evidenced by his desire to test the love of his daughters in a public arena but we are given no direct justification for the hatred unleashed against him by Goneril and Regan: we are left to ponder the cause of such family breakdown.

[104] Ibid., p. 695.

Though Dmytryk counters the potentially two-dimensional nature of his hero by giving him a social conscience from the outset, this western reincarnation of Lear constructs a hero for whom a redemptive path has no appeal and who sins as much as he is sinned against. Devereaux's response to the polluting of his lands at the hands of the copper mining company sanctioned by the government is excessively violent, resulting in a western showdown between Devereaux's men and the mine workers. But just as Lear is forced to bow to the forces of a new order, Devereaux must ultimately deal with the problem through the courts, where his frontier justice is shown to be brutal and no longer acceptable to a community investing in the kind of law and order established by government institutions. During the course of the trial Devereaux's lynching of cattle thieves also comes to light:

VAN CLEVE: I now ask you, sir, do you remember the names Charlie Monger, Red Dog Johnson or Carlos Rameriez?
MATT DEVEREAUX: No.
VAN CLEVE: The incident may be too trivial to recall. But isn't it true that you summarily hanged three of these men on the afternoon of June 4th?
MATT DEVEREAUX: They were stealing my cattle!
VAN CLEVE: I thought you didn't remember them.
MATT DEVEREAUX: I didn't ask their names!
VAN CLEVE: You just hanged 'em?
MATT DEVEREAUX: By the neck until they were dead. They were thieves!

Devereaux's acts of barbarism cannot be sanctioned: as with Lear, his dogged fidelity to an older code of ethics cannot be sustained. The constantly conflicting values conventionally associated with the western, as a genre of order, create a film world in which there can never be a stable milieu. There is a sense of radical instability operating at a literal and an ideological level in both *Broken Lance* and *King Lear*, but in Shakespeare's play there is also an innate sense of textual instability, a purposeful denial of assured interpretive positions which generates a more complex, less definitive hero.

Through his exploration of the corruption and prejudice at the core of this newly established, superficially more cultured and civilised society, Dmytryk challenges its stability both within its historical cinematic context and that of his contemporary America – an America which, in the fifties, blacklisted him, hauling him before the House of Un-American Activities Committee. Devereaux's lynching of cattle thieves associates him with acts of savagery but his attitude towards the Native American Indian and to the land itself is less barbaric than that of the supposedly civilised government and its representatives. Married to a Comanche who becomes the film's voice of reason and compassion, and father of a mixed race son who emerges as the only male with any sustainable sense of honour, Devereaux stands against the prejudiced values and corrupt ethos of his society. Whilst Lear must acquire a social conscience by treading a redemptive path, Devereaux is constructed as a hero with a ready-made conscience; his fair treatment of impoverished Indians found stealing his cattle demonstrates his humanity though as a frontier man he remains inextricably implicated in the displacement of the Native American Indian despite this or his pledged allegiance to his Comanche wife and to the well-being of the land which he tries to protect from contamination. His spiritual connection with the land is inferred by the merging of his image with that of the lone wolf in the film's closing frames, aligning Devereaux with the land and its permanence. Yet neither Devereaux nor Lear re-emerge as the leaders of the communities they have laboured to create: Devereaux may be an enlightened man of savage leanings and Lear may be a repentant sinner but the worlds they represent no longer exist. Dmytryk's *Broken Lance* is an elegy to the dying of the west; Shakespeare's *King Lear* is an elegy to the demise of patriarchal power: each text in its own way explores the deconstruction of a particular brand of macho honour and maps the disintegration of masculinity as that power and identity inevitably subsides.

Yordan's story presents us with an exposé of prejudice; the narrative is filtered through Devereaux's mixed race son, Joe, and the closing moments focus on Joe's departure from the prejudice-laden lands his father helped to tame. A romantic Hollywood-style closure is ensured through the union of Joe and the governor's daughter; they drive off not on horseback but in a horsedrawn buggy, Joe having relinquished his former cowboy image. His dramatic act of breaking the lance adorning Devereaux's grave and replacing it with flowers symbolises the end of his affiliation with the violence of the western frontier, as does his leave-taking with the Eastern educated Barbara who becomes synonymous with yet another new world in which prejudice plays no part.

However, despite being confined by expected Hollywood closure Dmytryk's film leaves us with an overall sense of this world's instability and little faith in the notion that the 'half-breed' Joe and his partner will escape society's prejudice given that it is a continuing presence in America in the fifties when the film was made. Just as the close of Shakespeare's tragedy leaves us with a feeling that the re-established order is precarious, any sense of equilibrium in this frontier landscape remains tentative. The 'strong lance of justice' (4.6: 162) still breaks, especially when it is associated with the kind of 'gold-plated sin' epitomised by the new orders which prevail in both Lear's and Devereaux's world. Whilst the western may resemble the heritage genre so often employed by adapters of Shakespeare to screen in terms of its mythical qualities, in *this* instance its mythical properties do not become synonymous with the kind of collective nostalgia we associate with heritage cinema. Heritage cinema can be overwhelmed by its nostalgic pre-occupation with the past, to the detriment of the social critiques and ironies embedded in the source texts such cinema is adapted from: the visual aesthetic often romanticises the past to the extent that the social criticism at the core of the narrative is subsumed.[105] But the writers and director of *Broken Lance* ensure that their own ideological concerns are not overwhelmed by either the nostalgic propensities of the western genre or its formulaic demands by incorporating a critique of social issues of pertinence to its US contemporary production climate, and in so doing they create connections with the social critiques embedded in Shakespeare's play. The film mirrors Shakespeare's *King Lear* at an ideological and a thematic level: each text explores issues of identity related to personal, familial and societal disintegration, presenting a violent yet melancholic elegy to the passing of a particular kind of existence.

King Lear *and the urban gangster movie: the 'tragic' gangster*

Although the gangster genre's affiliations with Shakespeare may seem tenuous, there are intriguing parallels to be drawn between this cinematic genre and both Elizabethan and Jacobean tragedy. The narrative styles and the archetypes employed in the gangster

 [105] Andrew Higson, *Waving the Flag: Constructing a National Cinema in Britain* (Oxford: Clarendon Press, 1995), p. 109.

movie mirror certain facets of the storytelling strategies adopted by Shakespeare and his theatrical contemporaries. Moreover, gangster movies revel in the kind of male-dominated violence and excessive body counts common in Elizabethan and Jacobean tragedy, and both genres overlap in terms of their ideologies and themes, especially when coupled with notions of revenge. The rise and fall narrative trajectory of the *classic* gangster film[106] – the codes and conventions of which are intrinsically connected to the American thirties – forms a recognisable part of the narrative patterning of numerous Elizabethan and Jacobean tragedies, from Christopher Marlowe's *Tamburlaine* to Shakespeare's *Macbeth*.

However, there are also fascinating textual transactions at work within post-thirties gangster films which are characterised by their preoccupation with both 'the family', in terms of its immediate and its wider 'mafia family' screen representation, and with the role of the patriarch within these families. In this context, the relationship between Shakespeare's *King Lear* and certain gangster films which emerge as tragic familial epics of a different type to the classic thirties gangster variety comes to the fore, leading us into as yet uncharted critical territory concerning the ways in which a text like *King Lear* cannot only be reconfigured as gangster epic but can also reshape the codes and conventions of the gangster genre. The adaptational interaction between this Shakespearean tragedy and the gangster genre demonstrates the ways in which film adaptation is caught up in what Robert Stam terms a 'whirl of intertextual reference and transformation', each text 'generating other texts' as part of an ongoing dialogical process.[107]

---

[106] *The Public Enemy* (1931); *Little Caesar* (1931), *Scarface: The Shame of the Nation* (1932).

[107] Stam, in Naremore, p. 66.

When writing of the British gangster cycle prevalent from 1998 to 2001, Steve Chibnall notes that the narrative structure employed by the 'heavy' gangster film of this era is usually 'one of tragedy in the Shakespearean or Jacobean mode'.[108] Robert Murphy also highlights the connection between the Jacobean revenge tragedy and the British gangster genre, likening Jack Carter (*Get Carter*, 1970) to both John Webster's Flamineo from *The White Devil* and Vindice in Thomas Middleton's *The Revenger's Tragedy*; even if urban gangsters like Carter are 'not so self-consciously evil' as their Jacobean counterparts, the protagonists in each genre are seen to share certain traits and characteristics.[109] Gangster versions of Shakespeare's *Macbeth* neatly plot the archetypal rise and fall of the hero whose excesses preordain his demise: films like *Joe Macbeth* (1955), *Men of Respect* (1991), TV adaptation *Macbeth on the Estate* (1997), Geoffrey Wright's Melbourne-based gangland *Macbeth* (2006) and Nick Paton's *Macbeth*, currently in post production, place the narrative within an urban underworld and map the inevitable downfall of their over-reaching protagonists. Less obvious gangster renditions of Shakespeare's plays also exist. Robert Warshow notes the narrative parallels between seminal gangster classics *Public Enemy* (1931) and *Little Caesar* (1931), Francis Ford Coppola's *Godfather* trilogy and Shakespeare's *Richard III*.[110] In his seminal essay, '"Top of the World, Ma": *Richard III* and Cinematic Convention', James Loehlin claims that, though

108 Steve Chibnall, 'Travels in Ladland: The British Gangster Cycle, 1998–2001', in *The British Cinema Book*, 2nd edition, edited by Robert Murphy (London: BFI, 2001), p. 282.

109 Robert Murphy, 'A Revenger's Tragedy – *Get Carter*', in *British Crime Cinema*, edited by Steve Chibnall and Robert Murphy (London: Routledge, 1999), p. 132.

110 Robert Warshow, *The Immediate Experience* (New York: Athenium, 1970), pp. 127–133.

Richard Loncraine does not create a gangster-fuelled underworld setting for his *Richard III* (1995), his screen version follows closely the classic gangster formula. He suggests that the archetypal gangster is similar to the over-reaching Machiavellian anti-hero of Elizabethan tragedy with whom the audience initially identifies yet ultimately rejects as soon as its 'transgressive desire' is satisfied.[111] Both the gangster and his tragedic counterpart see themselves as the outsiders whose Machiavellian over-reaching is a consequence of being 'unfairly excluded from society',[112] and in this sense Shakespeare's Richard III shares clearly identifiable character traits and motivations with the classic gangster protagonist.

Furthermore, Neil Sinyard argues that some gangster movies 'consciously court' parallels with *Richard III*, again highlighting the interconnectedness of a whole host of intertexts at work in the creation of a screen adaptation. He cites the 1958 *Al Capone* biopic as a film that integrates moments from Shakespeare's play text, whilst Richard's 'behavioural strategies', characterised by what Sinyard terms 'chilling hypocrisy yet dazzling chutzpah', are adopted by Michael Corleone in *The Godfather* as we cut from the baptism of his Godchild to scenes of violent excess orchestrated at his command.[113] More overt connections are established in James Gavin Bedford's *The Street King* (2002); an ethnic-based gangster rendition of *Richard III*, its tag-line openly proclaims its

---

[111] James Loehlin, '"Top of the World, Ma": *Richard III* and Cinematic Convention', in *Shakespeare the Movie: Popularizing the Plays on Film TV and Video*, edited by Richard Burt and Linda Boose (London: Routledge, 2003), p. 78.

[112] Ibid., p. 78.

[113] Neil Sinyard, 'Shakespeare Meets *The Godfather*: The Postmodern Populism of Al Pacino's *Looking For Richard*', in *Shakespeare, Film, Fin de Siècle*, edited by Mark Thornton Burnett and Ramona Wray. (Houndmills: Macmillan Press Ltd., 2000), p. 67.

status as 'Shakespeare's *Richard III* in 21st century Los Angeles'. Though its referencing of the play is 'more parodic and citational than assimilative' according to Cartelli and Rowe,[114] the film's appropriation of elements of *Richard III* within a gangster template again demonstrates the ongoing and fertile intertextual relationship between this popular cinematic genre and the 'high art' works of Shakespeare.

Three seminal movies dating from the 1930s are regarded as the prototype of the gangster genre: *The Public Enemy* (1931), *Little Caesar* (1931) and *Scarface: The Shame of the Nation* (1932) represent the gangster 'classic'. All three films, produced before the censorious interventions of the Hays Code, deal with the violence and criminality of the hoodlum underworld in a manner which was to disappear from movie screens by the mid-1930s as a consequence of the code. Despite disclaimers placed in the opening and closing titles of these films, denouncing the gangster lifestyle they portray and aimed at distancing the studio from any association with the glorification of the anti-hero at the centre of these narratives, the bad guy's charismatic appeal always outweighs the consequences of his fall from grace. Though dressed up as a morality tale in which the bad guy always loses, his 'untrammelled individualism'[115] lends his persona a mythical quality which transcends his inevitable downfall and aligns him with the Machiavellian heroes of Elizabethan and Jacobean theatre: Marlowe's *Tamburlaine* and Shakespeare's *Macbeth* – and in some interpretations *Richard III* – are once more called to mind.

---

[114] Thomas Cartelli and Katherine Rowe, editors, *New Wave Shakespeare on Screen* (Oxford: Blackwell, 2007), p. 103.
[115] Langford, p. 138.

In certain critical circles, *King Lear* has been deemed, similarly, a morality play showing us a redemptive path strewn with promises of regeneration,[116] its message being much more positive than that of the early gangster films of the 1930s with their explicit disclaimers. However, cinematic offshoots of the play which adopt the gangster genre template, on the whole, tend to reflect its apocalyptic propensities and the darker messages expounded in the studio disclaimers rather than any kind of regenerative moral positioning. The 'gangster' Lears we are presented with do not follow the redemptive path with any real conviction; they remain, like Shakespeare's *King Lear* and screen Lears envisioned in both Peter Brook's *King Lear* (1971) and Akira Kurosawa's *Ran* (1985), studies in failed patriarchy. They are flawed patricians, flawed father figures within the confines of both their 'mafia' family and their immediate family. The classic gangster formula works successfully for the translation to screen of such Machiavellian Shakespearean over-reachers as Macbeth and Richard III, but the cinematic transformation of a hero like King Lear is more problematic. He is already the ultimate insider, and his rise and fall cannot be mapped out as an exercise in ambitious excess but in the wilful relinquishing of it: his redemptive leanings do not fit neatly into the same rise and fall narrative trajectory.

Dudley Andrew notes that the 'dialetic interplay between the aesthetic forms of one period and the cinematic forms of our own period' can produce the 'otherness and distinctiveness' of one text in another text through 'refraction' as opposed to 'realisation';[117]

---

[116] Maynard Mack, *King Lear in Our Time* (London: Methuen, 1966), p. 117.

[117] Dudley Andrew, 'Adaptation: Concepts in Film Theory', in *Film and Literature: An Introduction and a Reader*, edited by Timothy Corrigan (New Jersey: Prentice-Hall, 1999), p. 265.

the 'dialectic interplay' between *King Lear* and numerous post-thirties familial gangster films illustrates the way in which the tragedic aesthetic embodied in *Lear* is 'refract(ed)' in the populist cinematic gangster genre. Such films are not necessarily a 'realisation' of Shakespeare's play but consideration of their mutual interdependency, and of the ways in which Shakespeare is refracted in the gangster film, leads to fertile discussion of the parallels to be drawn between the two forms. Ramona Wray notes an increasing critical interest in film texts that have a more 'tangential' connection to Shakespeare's works: 'How, and with what ideological effects, is the Shakespearean reconfigured?' is now the pressing question.[118] One may also ask, in this instance, how, and with what ideological effects, is the gangster genre reconfigured when it appropriates *King Lear* as subtext? If we can consider certain film texts as gangster versions of *King Lear*, can we not also consider how such films' affiliations with the Shakespeare text have shaped the gangster genre templates they employ?

The gangster film that places family – both personal and political – at the core of its narrative patterning is indebted not only to the story template employed in Shakespeare's *King Lear*, but to its ideological premise and its humanising of the 'gangster-patriarch' at the centre of the tale. The head of the mafia family portrayed in such films as *The Godfather* is isolated not by his position as the ultimate interloper (as is the case for the anti-hero of the classic gangster film), but as a consequence of his position as patriarch: unable to separate the roles of father of his immediate family from those of his extended mafia family, the patriarch of the post-thirties gangster film is, like Lear, unable to function effectively in either. The

[118] Ramona Wray, 'Shakespeare on Film in the New Millennium', *Shakespeare* 3.2 2007, pp. 270–282.

gangster genre can be read as an 'allegory of both the allure and the potentially catastrophic consequences of untrammelled individualism',[119] and in this Lear, along with the likes of Macbeth and Marlowe's Tamburlaine, can be refigured as the archetypal gangster whose 'untramelled individualism' takes him on a path to self-destruction. Whilst Lear's path is construed as a redemptive one in many staged versions of *King Lear*, in screen versions, with the exception of Kozintsev's *Korol Lir*, the redemptive elements are excised, or are at least rendered ineffectual, and we are presented with a patriarch whose wilfulness and innate belief in his own power blinds him to the realities of his standing – a standing which is dependent upon his place within the hierarchy of the group. Gangster Lears present us with what Langford terms a 'performative contradiction of radical autonomy and dependency'.[120] Like the head of the mafia family, Lear sees himself as being in thrall to no one yet his 'selfhood' is 'constructed through the group'; the archetypal gangster's refusal to register the role of others as part of the idea of selfhood may be seen as 'regressive infantile fantasy', or confirmation of a psychotic personality disorder.[121] Either diagnosis may be equally applicable to Shakespeare's *King Lear*. Lear's desire to be safely placed within the confines of Cordelia's 'nursery' smacks of 'regressive infantile fantasy' and his violent excesses – demonstrated through exile of those who dare to question the wisdom of his actions and through his vitriolic verbal attacks upon his daughters – reveal his psychotic tendencies.

His rise to power is not part of the narrative trajectory but the mapping of his downfall can be successfully translated into the

[119] Langford, p. 138.
[120] Ibid., p. 142.
[121] Ibid., pp. 142–143.

gangster genre template, the archetypal heroes of each genre sharing common ground in terms of their patriarchal position and their personality traits. The gangster genre's hero, like his western counterpart, has an ambivalent relationship with the values of 'civilised' society, operating beyond the confines of the mainstream; we are dealing in the gangster movie with a criminal underworld which adheres to its own set of conflicting values, its own territorial hierarchies, creating a parallel 'country' that works outside the parameters of the 'civilised' and in which the mafia boss is king. In its preoccupation with the concept of family – both its inherent loyalties and its betrayals – the gangster genre offers a close resemblance to the *Lear* narrative. The so-called pursuit of family preservation invariably brings about not only the gangster's demise but that of the family he seeks to protect, just as Lear's division of his lands, though it may be construed as an attempt to ensure a trouble-free devolution of power, precipitates his own destruction and that of his family and his kingdom. The kingdoms within which the narratives unfold conform to the 'genre of order', in which the 'symbolic arena of action'[122] becomes the all-important backdrop to the ideological and territorial conflicts that ensue. The urban underworlds of the gangster movie inevitably stand in ideological opposition to the values of the legitimate world and in this sense explore the same kind of juxtaposition of conflicting values realised in both the western and *King Lear*, the latter exploring the clash between an old feudal order epitomised by Lear, Kent and Gloucester, and the emerging new order characterised by self-interest and synonymous with Goneril, Regan, Cornwall and Edmund.

The *Lear* myth resonates within a diverse range of gangster-related narratives, from the aforementioned genre films, to art

122 Schatz, in Braudy and Cohen, pp. 697–698.

house offerings like Jean-Luc Godard's *King Lear* (1987) in which King Lear becomes retired mafia boss and failed father-figure, Don Learo, to the recent gangster-inflected *King Lear in the Hood*, placed within the public domain via YouTube.[123] The relationship between Shakespeare's text and various gangster-related screen narratives is, like the conceptual prism of genre, constantly changing and evolving in response to the cultural and industrial climate of cinematic production. Grieveson, Sonnet and Stanfield claim that gangster films provide 'an articulation of shifting cultural desires and anxieties' in which the figure of the gangster is 'produced differently within historical intersections of cultural identity'; they are 'not simply narratives for telling stories of ahistorical, undimensional figures or gangs but sites of instability of wider cultural resonance',[124] and the very instability of the *Lear* text lends itself to such shifting cultural examinations of desire and anxiety. Nor should Warshow's claims that the gangster genre is confined to the rise-and-fall tale of the disenfranchised loner be taken as the measure of the gangster genre. Grieveson et al point out that Warshow's construction of the generic gangster archetype is limited because it is generated in response to just three films from the 1930s.[125]

Fred Gardaphé identifies three stages of development of the gangster genre within American popular culture, connecting each of these stages to the concept of family and the experiences of the Italian immigrant: the first stage begins with Al Capone and concludes with the Vietnam War; the second considers the genre

---

[123] *King Lear in the Hood*, YouTube, posted 1/6/2006 (4 mins, 25) accessed 10/1/08.
[124] Lee Grieveson, Esther Sonnet, and Peter Stanfield, *Mob Culture: Hidden Histories of the American Gangster Film* (Oxford: Berg, 2002), pp. 1–9.
[125] Ibid., p. 2.

as 'a vehicle for the telling of the Italian immigrants' own story'; the third engages in the parodying of the gangster figure as 'representative of their culture'.[126] In this system of categorisation, the themes of disintegration and destruction of the family, characterised by 'a son of the New World rebelling against a father from the Old World', form an integral part of the ideological framework of Gardaphé's first phase, whilst the second phase adopts a more personal approach to similar issues in which 'notions of American manhood' and the efficacy of a disintegrating patriarchy are confronted. Gardaphé notes the ultimate disintegration of the gangster's traditional sense of manhood in the final phase, citing the protagonist of *The Sopranos* as a gangster patriarch who questions his role as husband, father, son and gangster through breaking the gangster code of silence, using words rather than actions to examine his identity crisis.[127] Even the *fin de siècle* anxieties surrounding manhood epitomised by Tony Soprano refract elements of *King Lear*. The preoccupations at the centre of the *Lear* text are at least refracted if not realised in all three of these phases through examination of personal identity crises and the breakdown of patriarchy, suggesting that the ongoing adaptational interaction between the gangster genre and *King Lear* is not simply a matter of how Lear's story is shaped in accordance with the cinematic codes and conventions of the gangster genre, but of how the gangster genre is in some respects shaped by the mythical *Lear* narrative, whether at a conscious or a subconscious level.

[126] Fred L Gardaphé, *From Wiseguys to Wisemen: The Gangster and Italian American Masculinities* (New York: Routledge, 2006), p. 12.

[127] Ibid., pp. 12–19.

Displacing the patriarchal family: Joseph Mankiewicz's House of Strangers (1949)

Although, with hindsight, Joseph Mankiewicz's *House of Strangers* is classified as a *film noir*, its affiliations with the genre tend to support the notion that *noir* is more an expression of style than a genre with a fixed narrative template and stock archetypes. James Naremore argues that *noir* is 'one of the most amorphous categories in film history': it could 'constitute a period, a genre, a cycle, a style, or simply a "phenomenon".'[128] Its emergence marks the marrying of the stylistic techniques of German expressionism with the pulp fiction narratives of the hard-boiled detective story but *House of Strangers* is based on the family drama *I'll Never Go There Again*, a novel written by Jerome Weidman. Max Monetti emerges as the ambivalent protagonist of the film, displaying some of the characteristic traits of the *noir* hero, but the storyline's continued preoccupation with notions of family, loyalty, honour and the clashes between an old world order and the values of a new world suggest its thematic associations lie more within the realms of the gangster genre than with *film noir*, despite the 'legitimate' nature of the business conducted by self-made immigrant father-figure, Gino Monetti, who heads the Monetti Bank and the Monetti household. We enter the narrative at the point when the autocratic Gino is at the height of his powers. However, the narrative trajectory plots his downfall and the subsequent rise of three of his sons, who have formerly been subjected to their father's disdain. The efforts of these power-hungry brothers are thwarted by a fourth son – Max, the youngest, favoured child – but he is unable ultimately to 'save' his overbearing father.

[128] Naremore, James. *More Than Night: Film Noir in its Contexts* (Berkeley, Los Angeles, London: University of California, 1998), pp. 9–11.

House of Strangers takes us into a world of dimly-lit urban backstreets and seedy nightclubs, Max's shabby office, housed within the halls of the Monetti Bank, offering a stark contrast to the bank's opulence. The costuming and iconography is redolent with *noir* imagery and Max is attracted to Irene, a 'dangerous' beauty of *noir*-like edginess. However, though Irene is positioned as the 'other' woman who lures Max away from his family commitment to marry the good Italian girl chosen for him by his father, she does not meet our expectations of the *femme fatale*. Instead, she represents rejection of the patriarchal control of the immigrant father figure and the traditions of the Old World. *Noir* narratives do, on occasion, involve the 'displacement of the patriarchal family'[129] and the tensions within this dysfunctional family become the main narrative thrust of *House of Strangers*, but the film does not fit with the conventions of the Hollywood thriller *noir* of the forties which tend to focus on morally flawed or psychologically damaged individuals.[130] Despite some of the ambiguities in his character, Max remains the Cordelia-like good son who stands in opposition to his materialistic brothers. Foster Hirsh notes that the film has two antecedents – biblical references to Joseph and his brothers and *King Lear*[131] but there are also intriguing intertextual connections to the western *Broken Lance*, Coppola's *Godfather* trilogy, the novels of Weidman and Mario Puzo, as well as Shakespeare's play and a range of genres across an extended period of cinematic history.

Although Max is constructed as the hero of the film we are drawn to the overbearing yet charismatic father figure, Gino Monetti, throughout the narrative. He is the working class immigrant

129 Ibid., p. 221.

130 Ibid., p. 222.

131 Foster Hirsh, DVD commentary, *House of Strangers* (1949).

who has realised the American Dream – the figure-head of the Monetti Bank – and he becomes the 'psychologically static' embodiment of a fixed 'world view', his immigrant mindset harbouring his 'unchanging cultural position'.[132] His is a story of 'wild self assertion' and 'radical self-fashioning'[133] on a par with that of the seminal gangsters of the 1930s, and the casting of Edward G. Robinson serves to further underline the gangster connection.[134] However, his role within the narrative is that of domineering patriarch: like Lear, he rules his 'kingdom' and his family, demanding loyalty and delivering edicts.

The opening moments of the film, photographed on location, present a series of exterior shots of the Lower East Side from which Gino has risen. Urban hustle and bustle dominates the frame and the sense of place is firmly established. Shot on location rather than on a studio set, the urban location is established as central to this narrative. From the landscape of the immigrant East Side we move to the 'civilised' seat of finance, visually highlighting Gino's rise from the Lower East Side to the architecture of the corporate world he comes to inhabit. But whilst we hear of Gino's rise to power through his egotistical recollections, the narrative focuses on his ultimate downfall in much the same way as both the narrative structure of the gangster genre and Shakespeare's *King Lear* map the inevitable demise of the father figure.

132 Schatz, p. 695.

133 Langford, p. 142.

134 Edward G. Robinson was, by the late 1940s, associated with the archetypal gangster: his lead role in the seminal gangster film, *Little Caesar*, was followed by similar performances in six gangster movies before the release of *House of Strangers*, establishing his persona with that of the gangster hero in the mind of his audience.

The film's trailer foregrounds Gino Monetti, the voice-over telling us that 'he built his empire from the gutter up' and that 'those who live under his roof are all strangers in the house of their mother, for the sins of their father have torn them apart,' turning Marina's 'house of love' into a 'house of strangers'. The moralistic tone of the trailer is similar to that of the disclaimers employed in the opening moments of the early thirties gangster films, its message in *House of Strangers* being that money and power can lead to emotional bankruptcy of the kind realised by Gino Monetti and, by inference, King Lear. However, the redemptive strands of the *Lear* narrative are sacrificed to the moral of this film's tale, and Gino remains a man isolated by his own wrong-doing. Barry Langford argues that a Marxist reading of the gangster genre stresses 'the notion of self alienation as an irradicable function of capitalism', resulting in the inevitable 'corruption of the family';[135] given the film trailer's condemnation of Gino, his 'self alienation' and his 'corruption of the family', similar claims can be made for *House of Strangers*. When Gino faces a prison sentence due to his illegal banking practices, his sons, with the exception of Max, refuse to stand by him since he has treated them so harshly during their lifetime; Gino proclaims, 'For a few dollars a week I coulda had a good son', thus reducing the sum of their emotional commitment to a monetary level and demonstrating how the capitalistic advancement he has pursued in the name of the family has inevitably corrupted it.

Gino plays the domineering patriarch within the confines of his own home. Its palatial grandeur is overly opulent and claustrophobic, the operatic strains of *The Barber of Seville* (another tale of a self-made man who, like Monetti, built up an empire against

135 Langford, p. 141.

the odds) blasting out discomfortingly from the gramophone at Gino's command and demonstrating the way in which he pervades every aspect of the family's existence. The parallels between the overbearing Gino and the petulant King Lear are clearly drawn as are their demands for acquiescence from their offspring. And, like Lear, Gino's 'psychologically static' persona leads to a self-willed denial of the changes taking place around him. When Gino first enters the frame in his chauffeur-driven car his regal presence is acknowledged by the crowd that surrounds his bank. His name is engraved into the stonework of the building and his portrait dominates the banking hall where petitioners cue up for a personal audience with him. He doles out monetary favours in an arbitrary fashion, making much of his own benevolence as he gives money to a woman who needs cash to pay for her son's medical care, yet proceeds to charge exorbitant interest rates to a struggling immigrant worker. Although his dealings are conducted within a legitimised system, his *modus operandi* has much in common with those of the mafia bosses found in gangster movies who grant or deny favours to their clientelle; indeed, the opening moments of both *The Godfather* and *The Godfather II* echo these scenes from *House of Strangers* as the Dons bestow favours to waiting petitioners.

In stark contrast to the grandeur of his initial arrival at the bank, Gino is later swamped by rioting investors who are protesting against the government closure of the bank due to its improper trading practices. His emotional investment in the ways of the old world and the old ways of conducting business brings the family empire crashing down. Failure to comply with the rules and regulations being introduced within this emerging capitalistic world – a world he is unable and unwilling to engage with due to his unchanging cultural position – sets him apart and the film continues to map the demise of his empire as we witness the dramatic removal of his name from the architecture of the bank, the old order visibly being replaced by the new, with a sign noting the names of his sons now dominating the frame. Gino, like Lear, is cast out into a parallel wilderness, a castrated patrician for whom death is the only natural progression. The final drama, in which Max confronts his brothers on his release from jail, gives the film a potentially Jacobean twist in the closing moments as Joe tries to kill Max and Pietro kills Joe, but the body count and the violence are minimal and, in line with the forties Hollywood studio system, closure is neat and 'happy' as we return to the romantic story line, Max and Irene driving off into the sunset.

Mafia father figures: Francis Ford Coppola's The Godfather trilogy (1972, 1974, 1990)

Despite the hero status of Max Monnetti and the fact that much of the film's screen time is devoted to his love interest with Irene, *House of Strangers* remains Gino's story. What is also apparent to the modern cinema-going audience are the parallels between this film and the narrative strands which run through *The Godfather* trilogy: the theme of the immigrant's rise to a position of authority, the harking back to the traditions of the old country, the significance of family, its honour, its loyalties and its inherent betrayals are sewn into the fabric of the narrative of *House of Strangers* and all three *Godfather* films. The financial successes of the increasingly big budget Paramount studio productions of *The Godfather* and *The Godfather II* placed tremendous pressure on Coppola to create a final act to his narrative, with *The Godfather III* closing the trilogy. Much has been made of the connections between *King Lear* and *The Godfather III*; by the time Coppola is coerced into making the third *Godfather* film he is seen to appropriate *King Lear* as a means of investing the tired story line with the required 'grandeur',[136] but the narrative patterning in *House of Strangers* and *each* of the *Godfather* films suggests that connections with both Mankiewicz's film and *King Lear* are more closely drawn across the trilogy as a whole.

What ties the films and their particular textual transactions to Shakespeare's play are their shared thematic and ideological preoccupations: we have a performance space and a film world of contested spaces in which society's values are in flux, violent social disintegration being a direct consequence; we have 'families' led by domineering patriarchs who, in pursuit of family preservation, engender the family's downfall from within; and notions of family honour and loyalty tested against a backdrop of deception and betrayal of decidedly tragedic Jacobean proportions. Direct familial connections to *King Lear* within this narrative are less overt: Don Vito Corleone has four sons (one of whom is adopted into the family) and a daughter. However, there remain echoes of Lear's family situation. We have the division between 'bad' sons (Fredo) and 'good' sons, with Michael Corleone taking the role of favoured younger child who returns from a self-imposed exile to take his place, somewhat reluctantly, within the family business, and similarly, in *Godfather III*, we have a favoured, younger daughter and a son ostracised from the family.

Just as Weidman viewed his novel as a family drama, *The Godfather* is, according to its author, Mario Puzo, 'a family novel rather than a crime novel', his don more of an 'old patriarch who makes the world safe for his beloved family' than the 'foul-mouthed, blood-thirsty thug of previous gangster books and movies'.[137] Coppola also claims that the film trilogy explores his

---

[136] Howard, in Jackson, p. 297.

[137] Michael Schumacher, *Francis Ford Coppola: A Filmmaker's Life* (New York: Bloomsbury, 1999), p. 89.

preoccupation with the importance of family in modern society; it is a family epic spanning more than seventy years, addressing 'questions of power and succession' within the patriarchal structures of 'the family';[138] the Corleone family's story is no different 'from the stories of such families as the Kennedys or the Rothschilds, each founded by powerful, influential patricians, each experiencing both subtle and dramatic changes as one generation (is) succeeded (by) its predecessor'.[139] Marlon Brando saw Don Corleone as 'a kind of hero ... a man of substance, tradition, dignity, refinement, a man of unerring instinct who just happened to live in a violent world',[140] and his performance reflects his more complex and humane reading of this mafia father figure. Earlier notions of the gangster as 'social deviant' are revised in favour of a 'humanised' gangster, redefined as a 'cultural hero' by many.[141] Within the social context of seventies America, *The Godfather* and *The Godfather II* explore the ways in which American masculinity has been affected by the cultural power shifts engendered by the rise of feminism.[142] In response to challenges to American manhood and the disappearance of effective patriarchal structures, screen figures like the Godfather are culturally legitimised because they offer a fictional return to a traditional, patriarchal sense of manhood. Perhaps, as Michael Schumacher suggests, the success of the first two films is a consequence of society's willingness to 'embrace a more rigid, almost Machiavellian leadership in exchange for order in the house' at the end of 'one of America's

---

[138] Francis Ford Coppola interviewed in *Heart of Darkness: A Film-maker's Life*. Online: www.filmreference.com/Directors-Bu-Co/Coppola-Francis-Ford.html

[139] Schumacher, p. 156.

[140] Ibid., p. 115.

[141] Gardaphé, pp. 22–31.

[142] Ibid., p. 42.

most turbulent decades';[143] but like Lear, Don Vito Corleone and his successor, Michael, are the last bastions of effective patriarchal power operating in a world that also expresses its discomfort with notions of patriarchal dominance and control.

As with *King Lear*, we first enter Don Corleone's world at a point when he is feeling the weight of leadership rather than with the classic gangster film's conventional tracking of the protagonist's rise to glory. The opening moments of play text and film text also present us with a parallel situation: Don Corleone holds court as petitioners line up to request favours from him on the day of his daughter's wedding; Lear holds court ostensibly to arrange the marriage of Cordelia to suitors France or Burgundy, but has the covert agenda of granting favours through the division of his territories. In both situations, they emerge as powerful, patriarchal figures of seemingly benevolent intent, presiding over portentous celebratory moments connected to family: but neither Lear nor Corleone can separate the role of father from that of patriarch in its wider context. This narrative patterning established at the start of *The Godfather* is also revisited in both *Godfather* sequels, Don Corleone's role being taken up by his successor, Michael, who seems to transform from wilful favoured child of Cordelia-like proportions in *The Godfather* to the new pseudo-Lear figure in *The Godfather II*. Just as Don Corleone presides over the granting of favours in the first film's opening frames, Michael is petitioned for assistance by Rocco Lampone who kisses the hand of this 'young prince, recently crowned king',[144] whilst beyond the confines of his office the Corleone family are again seen engaging in a family-

[143] Schumacher, p. 93.

[144] Mario Puzo and Francis Ford Coppola, *Screenplay: The Godfather II* (2nd draft September 1973). Online: www.awesomefilm.com/script/godfather2html

oriented celebration, this time in attendance at Michael's son's communion and party. Similarly, we open with a ceremony and celebratory family party in *The Godfather III* as Michael Corleone is granted the Order of St Sylvester for outstanding service to the Catholic church, one such service echoing Lear's gifting of lands. Such intertextual allusions to *King Lear* are threaded into the fabric of the trilogy as a whole, as are references to other Shakespearean tragedies and histories.[145] Consequently, each film is given some of the mythical grandeur of Shakespeare's play.

However, what is most striking is the way in which Coppola underlines the mythical proportions of the father-figure within the Corleone dynasty by cutting from the family business and cele-brations in the opening moments of *The Godfather II* to a flashback narrative detailing the miraculous escape of Vito Corleone from his native Sicily; the Sicilian landscape opens on a very different kind of family ceremony, this time a funeral procession in which 'the figures move slowly, seemingly from out of hundreds of years of the past'.[146] The language of the screenplay is redolent with mythical weight, lending the moment a fable-like quality, and setting up Vito Corleone as a child with a charmed life. He becomes synonymous with the immigrant's rise-against-all-odds scenario as images of immigrant families 'huddled together with all their earthly posses-sions on their way to America' are juxtaposed with that of New York harbour as 'we glide past the Statue of Liberty',[147] icon of hope and future prosperity.

---

[145] *The Godfather* also alludes to *Henry V*, *Macbeth* and *Richard III*: Michael Corleone can be seen as a pseudo-Hal who returns to his pre-ordained 'duties', an ambitious over-reacher, and a cunning strategist as suggested by Neil Sinyard in 'The Postmodern Populism of *Looking for Richard*'.

[146] Puzo and Coppola, *Screenplay: Godfather II*.

[147] Ibid.

By the seventies, the makers of gangster movies were no longer forced into taking a moral stand in opposition to the mobster lifestyle, leaving Puzo and Coppola free to invest their archetypal gangster hero with a sense of old world honour and justice: he is the immigrant who has made good by the only means open to him in this new world and he remains a 'benefactor of the powerless'[148] within his neighbourhood through a route less legal yet not dissimilar to that taken by Gino Monetti. Notions of justice permeate *The Godfather* trilogy and *King Lear*. Whilst Lear must journey towards a realisation of what constitutes justice, Don Corleone is invested with the power to implement justice for the Italian immigrant in his world from the film's outset, legitimate routes of the new country failing to exact the required revenge. When asking the Don to avenge a brutal attack upon his daughter, Bonasera says, 'I went to the police like a good American' but 'for true justice ... we must go to The Godfather'.

These texts also share a preoccupation with redemption – a characteristic far from the conventional realms of the classic gangster movie in which the rise and the inevitable fall of the archetypal hero is a given. Don Vito Corleone is resistant to the family's association with money procured through drugs and prostitution, and he retains the old world values of his Sicilian upbringing within the Catholic church, despite the more violent actions he must perform in order to retain control of his mafia family. He is out of sync with the new families who wish to enter the aforementioned branches of underworld crime and – as with Lear – it is, in part, his resistance to the new order that ensures his demise. Despite the violence and the Henry V-like nature of his earlier rise to power, Michael's redemptive desires are foregrounded prominently

[148] Schumacher, p. 89.

at the close of *The Godfather II* when he states 'All my life I wanted out', echoing Lear's desire to relinquish control of his kingdom. Unlike the stock archetype of the gangster genre, whose world view according to Schatz is 'static' and unchanging,[149] Michael actively seeks to change his view and his position within the world. His redemptive attempts to legitimise the family business are set in motion in *Godfather II* but are realised in *Godfather III* when he sells off the family's casinos and buys into the seemingly legitimate Immobilaire, an old, respected European company in which the Vatican has a considerable financial stake and that is, ironically, eventually exposed as a corrupt institution. Michael's redemptive path is, however, blocked at every turn not only in this respect but also in terms of his capacity to protect his immediate family who, like Lear's daughters, conspire against him at various times. His opening voiceover in *The Godfather III* states 'I would burn in hell to keep you safe', but it is his dissolution of his mafia family that brings about the death of his daughter, Mary, and the eventual demise of the Corleone empire. By trying to extricate himself from his gangster persona – just as Lear attempts to extricate himself from the burdens of state – Michael precipitates his own downfall, denying his dependency upon the mafia family to which his identity is intrinsically linked. The closing image of the Don shows him a lonely, isolated old man who keels over unceremoniously.

There have been many deaths *en route* during the course of the trilogy's narrative but, in the moments prior to the Don's uneventful death scene, the film plays to its Jacobean strengths in a frenzy of revenge attacks. The family's attendance at the opera house is intercut with scenes of Vincent Corleone – son of Sonny and rising star of the Corleone family – wreaking revenge on conspirators of

---

[149] Schatz, p. 695.

the Immobilaire scam: the corrupt archbishop and the traitor Don Lucrezzi meet a bloody end and Don Atobello suffers the ultimate Jacobean fate of death by poisoning as he eats the cakes Michael's sister has prepared for him in a macabre act of family revenge. The final showdown on the steps of the opera house presents us with a highly emotive, theatrical moment, borrowing heavily from the *Lear* text; the grieving king's 'Howl! howl! howl! howl!' (5.3: 255) permeates the frame as Mary dies in the arms of her grief-stricken father, freighting it with the dramatic weight of prior stage and screen performances of *King Lear*.

This last film in the trilogy may lack the critical acclaim enjoyed by its predecessors but, in its ambitious attempts to place the Corleone family saga firmly within the realms of tragedy, it achieves considerable success. Michael Corleone's narrative trajectory is finally realised: whilst his initial gangster fate has more in common with Shakespearean protagonists like the ambitious over-reacher, Macbeth, he emerges during the course of *The Godfather III* as a man who, like Lear, seeks redemption and forgiveness. The close of the trilogy is, however, infused with the same sense of foreboding that seeps into the closing moments of *King Lear*. In both texts we have newly legitimised beginnings, but as audiences we remain unconvinced of their stability and aware of their propensity for future corruption.

Gangster Lear *as morality tale: Don Boyd's* My Kingdom *(2001)*

Don Boyd's *My Kingdom* is not the only recent British gangster film to employ *King Lear* as subtext: John Irvin's *Shiner*, released in 2000, shares the play's preoccupation with familial betrayal and the demise of the father figure, and the suspicious death of Billy Shiner's favoured son, possibly as a consequence of the actions of one of his evil daughters, echoes the *Lear* narrative and its archetypal template. However, it is the immigrant experience explored in both *House of Strangers* and *The Godfather* trilogy that links the founding fathers of these American gangster movies with Don Boyd's British gangster film, *My Kingdom*. The founding father of each of these dynasties comes from an underclass that has succeeded against the odds in a land of greater opportunity. In *My Kingdom*, the Sicilian-born New Yorker is superseded by the Irish interloper whose land of opportunity becomes the supposedly wealthier docklands of a contemporary Liverpool, basking in its former colonial glory – a 'great city' of 'steam ships' and 'iron shavings' according to protagonist Sandeman in a rare moment of nostalgic reflection before his world is plunged into chaos.

As with *House of Strangers* and *The Godfather*, we enter the narrative at a point where the film's protagonist, Sandeman, is seemingly at the height of his powers: he is in control of both his 'mafia' family and his direct family, which consists of a much-loved wife, two errant daughters, and the obligatory youngest favourite. But in *My Kingdom* it is the death of Sandeman's wife that precipitates his downfall in a psychological sense, exposing his weaknesses and leaving him vulnerable to attack from within. The narrative charts his downfall as his power-hungry daughters and their partners seek control, and we are led to the inevitable destruction of the underworld empire Sandeman has created.

The significance of place is again made abundantly clear as the opening shots reveal the cityscape and docklands of a contemporary Liverpool. For director Don Boyd, Liverpool functions 'not just as a background'; here, place is 'integral to the story',[150] its 'profile in history'[151] adding extra layers to the film's subtext.

---

[150] Don Boyd, DVD commentary, *My Kingdom* (2001).

[151] Producer, audio commentary, *My Kingdom* (2001).

Courtney Lehmann argues that Boyd 'privileges place as a means of direct engagement with a present whose identity has been eroded by the centrifugal energies of globalisation, the paranoia of a post 9/11 culture, an imploding neglect and, above all, the fear that the apocalypse has already arrived'.[152] Her critique invests the film with a political agenda, its setting becoming synonymous with 'the spectre of long-term cataclysmic decline'[153] and the kind of inevitable nihilism with which many stage productions and screen versions of King Lear have become associated from the late twentieth century onwards. Lehmann claims that Boyd's depiction of Liverpool as a site of 'broken promises of urban renovation' functions as an exposé of the ways in which global capitalism preys upon humanity and thus connects the predatory nature of twenty-first century capitalism with Lear's world in which 'humanity must perforce prey upon itself'.[154] However, Lehmann also highlights the regenerative propensities embedded in the film, its 'almost total nihilism' performing 'its own kind of urban "renovation"',[155] and offering, it would seem, the kind of regenerative possibilities envisaged at the close of Edward Bond's stark socialist adaptation of the Lear narrative in his stage play Lear.

Whilst the political ideologies seen by Lehmann to be at the core of the film remain a question of interpretation, its function as a morality tale is more overt. Despite the moralising attached to seminal gangster films of the thirties, through clumsy and unconvincing

---

[152] Courtney Lehmann, 'The Postnostalgic Renaissance: The "Place" of Liverpool in Don Boyd's My Kingdom', in Screening Shakespeare in the Twenty-first Century, edited by Mark Thornton-Burnett and Ramona Wray (Edinburgh: Edinburgh University Press, 2006), pp. 72–73.

[153] Ibid., p. 73.

[154] Ibid., p. 73.

[155] Ibid., p. 73.

disclaimers and the inevitable fall of the over-reaching gangster hero, the glamorisation of the gangster lifestyle and the protagonist's charismatic appeal prevails. In *My Kingdom* Boyd is at pains to distance himself from any kind of romanticising of the gangster image and seeks instead, against the genre's *classic* conventions, to explore the 'moral complexities' of a gangster patriarch such as Sandeman.[156] As with the Sicilian Godfathers, Irish immigrant Sandeman is seen to retain his connections to the church, Liverpool's cathedral becoming a symbol for the morality at the core of the narrative as it takes on an iconic architectural significance within the film. The opening images of Liverpool's dockside are juxtaposed alongside panning shots of the cathedral, the streets below the shadows of this grand structure harbouring prostitutes and drug addicts. Despite the violent excesses of the script – in which the psychotic Jug's sadistic acts are frequently given screen prominence – and its inclusion of a key scene in which Sandeman disrespectfully brokers a drugs deal via mobile phone during a church service, the custodians of the cathedral agreed to filming inside the building, maintaining that Boyd is taking a very 'moral position' about the people involved.[157] Sandeman's journey towards some kind of Lear-like redemption provides the film's narrative momentum and the closing moments of the film witness the demise of his adversaries, leaving the villains either dead or arrested. He becomes the British gangster film's 'wronged man pursuing justice',[158] avenging his own betrayal. The values of civilised society *appear* to be upheld, order is restored and Jo – unlike Cordelia – lives on, maintaining the film's moral centre.

[156] Don Boyd, DVD commentary, *My Kingdom* (2001).

[157] Ibid.

[158] Steve Chibnall and Robert Murphy, 'Parole overdue: releasing the British crime film into the critical community', in *British Crime Cinema*, edited by Steve Chibnall and Robert Murphy (London: Routledge, 1999), p. 4.

However, Boyd infuses his film with the kinds of moral ambiguities found in Shakespeare's *King Lear*. Sandeman's grandson, constructed as pseudo-Fool, becomes synonymous with innocence which, by the close of the film, is sacrificed unceremoniously, his callous murder mirroring that of the play's hanged Cordelia. The boy also becomes a pseudo-Cordelia, affecting her *moral* presence in her *material* absence in much the same way as the Fool in Shakespeare's *King Lear* is often played as a manifestation of Lear's estranged daughter. Sandeman's relationship with this child provides his pathway to redemption; homeless, cast out on the docklands with only his grandson, Sandeman comes to the realisation that it is more important to be seen as 'the man' by this boy than by the mafia family which has ultimately ejected him.

Echoes of the reconciliation scene between Lear and Cordelia saturate the film text and when Sandeman finds the body of the murdered child, his howls evoke the cultural memory of former stage and screen moments from both *King Lear* and the closing moments of *Godfather III*. Vindicated in part by his involvement in the capture of the gangster family members he once protected, and reconciled with his good daughter, Jo, Sandeman remains the isolated hero of the genre of order, unable to re-assimilate or to accept the values of either the civilised world or those of an underworld in flux. He is dead in all but a physical sense: his identity, so closely linked to that of his gangster family, is shattered and his place within the traditional family is untenable. He is a cipher, a nothing, the moral of the tale being realised as he is seen drifting off into the dockland landscape in the film's final frames. Contrary to Lehmann's reading of the film text as a site of regenerative possibilities, the closing moments present us with an image of a defeated patrician cast out into the unstable wilderness of a bleak twenty-first-century Liverpool, echoing only the apocalyptic sentiment found in screen visions of *King Lear* already produced by Peter Brook (*King Lear*, 1971) and Akira Kurosawa (*Ran*, 1985).

Directorial reference to *King Lear* appears in the closing credits. 'From a story by Don Boyd, inspired by William Shakespeare's *King Lear*': it is not, according to Boyd, an adaptation of the play, the story's links to the *Lear* narrative being secondary to its exploration of Liverpool as a 'society in moral decline'.[159] And yet, of all cinematic off-shoots of *King Lear*, whether rooted in the gangster genre, the western, the jidai-geki genre, road movie or melodrama, Boyd's *My Kingdom* bears closest resemblance to Shakespeare's play in terms of its thematic and ideological preoccupations, its structural parallels and its character frameworks. Boyd's film draws upon the narrative structure of *King Lear*, demonstrating in the process not only the ways in which Shakespeare's tragedy translates with ease into the gangster genre template, but how the codes and conventions of the familial gangster epic are shaped in response to the ideological and thematic preoccupations of the play. *My Kingdom* is one of few screen adaptations of *King Lear* that realise on screen its inherent violence: initial scenes of sadistic torture are compounded throughout, culminating in the putting out of Quick's eyes, and a final body count of suitably Jacobean tragedic proportions. Boyd's archetypal heroes and villains are also carbon copies of those found in *King Lear* and unlike writer-directors of other gangster renditions of the narrative, he feels no compulsion to change the gender of his adversaries nor to excise the more overtly redemptive elements of Lear's psychological journeying.

Women in this gangster film – dominant, in control, independent – play against generic convention and the on-screen realisation of

---

[159] Don Boyd, DVD commentary, *My Kingdom* (2001).

Mandy Sandeman fleshes out the missing component of the Shakespearean text, reconfiguring the power-base as Lynn Redgrave infuses the role with a matriarchal might that permeates the film, despite her early demise. It is Mandy who dominates the opening scenes, who provides family unity: when family members are first introduced she is at the centre of all activity, orchestrating events and sharing moments of intimacy with her daughters and her grandson, whilst Sandeman sits alone playing patience, action scenes from three TV screens flickering constantly behind his prophetically inert frame. Her death signals the start of patriarchal disintegration within this film world and her absence reverberates throughout as the narrative unfolds, reminding us of an earlier time of order and stability. The egotistical Sandeman is unable to accept that her death is the result of a random act of violence: he concocts conspiracy theories, asking 'Who in God's name would mug me?' rather than accepting that the world he has helped to shape has also generated desperate drug addicted boys like Mandy's murderer, Delroy.

Sandeman is introduced as a man whose place at the head of the gangster hierarchy is uncontested yet he, like Lear, is already contemplating his own withdrawal having decided to appoint his youngest daughter as custodian of the family business a year before the film's narrative turning point – a point precipitated by the murder of his wife. There are numerous striking similarities between the film text and play at such structural levels, and despite Boyd's assertion that *King Lear*'s function is secondary to that of his Liverpool setting, he co-opts the play in ways which are far more explicit than any other cinematic genre renditions to date. The reading of the will works as a parallel moment to the division of the land in *King Lear*, both scenes encapsulating the political dynamics of the narrative. Boyd separates the love test from the division, turning Mandy's wake into a macabre display of show and tell grief with Sandeman's eldest daughter, Kath, indulging in an insincere public declaration of love, in praise of family values and a 'wonderful' father – 'You we honour, you we obey, you we love' – whilst Tracey steals her glory with a tortuous karaoke rendition of Barry Manilow's *Mandy*. However, the scene is intercut with graphic images of sadistic torture perpetrated by Tracey's partner, Jug, leading us to question the sincerity of these public displays of affection in much the same way as Cordelia's opening asides invite our scepticism. Through such visual means Boyd also demonstrates the impending decline of the patriarchal Sandeman: we cut from Sandeman and Desmond, father of Mandy's murderer, to scenes of the murderer's explicit torture – despite Sandeman's orders not to harm him, despite his reassurances to Desmond that the boy is safe. Once again, the values of the old criminal order, synonymous with Sandeman and Desmond, are superseded by a new order, devoid of the veneer of honour and integrity a church-going father-figure like Sandeman has lent to the criminal underworld.

The film's preoccupation with family, with matters of love, honour, deception, and betrayal draws obvious parallels with the *Lear* narrative in much the same way as its gangster predecessors. However, Boyd's film offers a much closer exploration of the play's interrogation of the theme of justice; it becomes an integral part of Boyd's construction of this gangster kingdom. Detective Quick points out to Sandeman that the working class Delroys of this world are 'tragic' since the only way they can 'make it off the streets in Liverpool is through the entertainment industry, sport or crime'; but he also argues that Sandeman (and by associative inference King Lear) and '(his) kind' rob them of 'hope,' leading this gangster patrician to question his position. Moreover, it forces him to accept the earlier claims of his underworld rival, The Chair, who argues that

Sandeman, as the drug provider who breeds boys like Delroy, is responsible for the death of his own wife, and adds another tragic dimension to the film.

A Marxist reading of the film flags up the 'corruption of family' as a repeated motif of the gangster genre.[160] As with *House of Strangers*, this film's trailer highlights issues of power and money: it is set up as 'a conflict over a mother's legacy', in which 'a family battles for control of a kingdom', Jo stating that it is 'always about money'. And it is in pursuit of money and power, ostensibly for the good of the family, that gangster father figures like Sandeman ultimately destroy it, 'encapsulating the Marxist insight that the protected "familial" realm cannot finally be protected from the atomising forces of the very capitalism that claims to preserve it'.[161] Sandeman's pursuit of power and wealth culminates in the death of his wife and grandson, the destruction of his family and his ultimate self-alienation. The closing shot of a solitary, powerless Sandeman, wandering aimlessly in the docklands locale he once ruled, offers a stark visual contrast to the opening frames of the Liverpool landscape he dominated at the narrative's outset. According to Lehmann, *My Kingdom* is a 'post-nostalgia film' which, unlike so many heritage screen versions of Shakespeare's plays, engages with the present without evoking a 'sense of period' or nostalgic 'retreat into the past'.[162] However, whilst it may not offer a retreat into the past, it cannot avoid a sense of period since it is engaging in debate about the state of the nation as we move into the twenty-first century: like its gangster predecessors it dramatises 'the notion of self alienation as an irradicable function of capitalism', resulting in the inevitable 'corruption of the family'.[163] The

[160] Langford, p. 141.

[161] Ibid., p. 141.

[162] Lehmann, pp. 72–73.

[163] Langford, p. 141.

opening image of the solitary Sandeman playing patience stays with us, leading us not only to question the credibility of his position as ruthless twenty-first century gangster patrician from the outset, but to acknowledge the vulnerability of all patriachal structures, from that of despotic monarch or mafia patrician to father of the house, regardless of the era or the generic framework employed for narration of the tale.

Tony Howard argues that it is the western that 'reinstates Renaissance codes of masculinity and poetic justice'[164] but his contention is equally applicable to the gangster genre; the solitary hero of the western is replaced by the gangster over-reacher who seeks ultimate power and control yet remains reliant upon the group for his power *and* for his identity. In this respect the gangster archetype offers an even more fitting genre realisation of a protagonist like King Lear, whose persona is intrinsically linked to his place within the hierarchy. In cinematic off-shoots which adopt the gangster genre template, the gangster patrician's attempts to extricate himself from the burdens of leadership set in motion his downfall, mirroring closely both the character frameworks created in Shakespeare's *King Lear*, and the play's preoccupation with the dramatisation of the demise of patriarchal and familial institutions, whether situated in a legitimate world or an underworld.

What marks out the gangster scenario as the most fitting of genre templates for screen adaptations of *King Lear* is its propensity for violent excess and its interrogation of the kind of evil embodied in Shakespearean and Jacobean tragedy – an evil which 'must perforce prey upon itself like monsters of the deep' (4.2: 50–51); what marks out *King Lear* as the most fitting subtext for the type of tragic familial epic epitomised by such films as *House of Strangers*,

---

[164] Howard in Jackson, p. 297.

The Godfather trilogy, and *My Kingdom*, is its close examination of the father figure at the centre of disintegrating patriarchal power structures, of family and of kingdom. The textual transactions taking place between the genre of tragedy and the cinematic gangster genre demonstrate not only the hybridity of Shakespeare's narratives but their capacity to influence the codes and conventions of a certain type of gangster film.

King Lear *as melodrama: Jocelyn Moorhouse's* A Thousand Acres *(1997)*

Written by Laura Jones, an adept and prolific adapter of literary texts to screen,[165] *A Thousand Acres* (1997) presents Jane Smiley's revisionist version of Shakespeare's *King Lear* within the cinematic conventions of the melodrama. Whether we view Smiley's novel or Shakespeare's play as the film's source, its affiliation with the genre of melodrama is indisputable; the tagline, 'Best friends. Bitter rivals. Sisters', foregrounds the importance of its female protagonists within the context of family, and precipitates emotional excess.

Smiley's novel and Moorhouse's film adaptation is set in a 1970s Iowa farming community at the point when land baron, Larry Cook, is about to hand over control of his territory to his daughters and their respective partners. Whilst we are once more presented with two daughters with whom the father has a troubled relationship, and a favoured younger daughter, this narrative unfolds from the perspective of Cook's eldest child, Ginny, and it is her story of incestuous abuse that provides narrative momentum.

As with *film noir*, the issues surrounding melodrama as a genre continue to generate debate: it is a genre which is constantly

---

[165] Laura Jones adapted a further six literary classics during 1990–2002: *An Angel at My Table* (1990); *Portrait of a Lady* (1996); *The Well* (1997); *Oscar and Lucinda* (1997); *Angela's Ashes* (1999); *Possession* (2002).

redefined at a critical level, arguably part of *all* Hollywood narratives rather than a clearly delineated genre with a distinct set of codes and conventions specific to a particular type of film. Rick Altman claims that melodrama has 'a syntax but lacks a clear semantic dimension',[166] while Linda Williams sees it as a 'mode' or a 'tendency', its formal and stylistic motifs varying according to both its era of production and its medium.[167] Indeed, *A Thousand Acres* has been labelled pure 'soap opera'[168] in some critical circles and in a nineties context the parallels between the cinematic mode of melodrama and televised 'soap' are inevitable. The genre of melodrama, in its populist sense, is a narrative which foregrounds feminine experience, usually within a domesticated setting. But feminist theorists of the seventies have posthumously generated the acceptance of a gendered melodrama or woman's film, the characteristics of which are seen to invest the films with a subversive sub-textual energy. The works of such fifties Hollywood directors as Douglas Sirk thus become politicised and when read from a feminist perspective the woman's weepie, epitomised by its emotive and stylistic excess, becomes synonymous with a potentially subversive form of cinema.

The melodrama's preoccupation with the patriarchal institution of family, and to a lesser degree marriage, lends itself to certain aspects of the *Lear* narrative but the genre's traditional focus on the woman's position within the family offers a shift of perspective

---

[166] Rick Altman, 'Cinemas and Genres', in *The Oxford History of World Cinema*, edited by Geoffrey Nowell-Smith (Oxford: Oxford University Press, 1996), p. 282.

[167] Linda Williams, 'Melodrama Revised', in *Refiguring American Film Genres: Theory and History*, edited by Nick Browne (Berkeley: University of California, 1998), pp. 42–88.

[168] Mick LaSalle, '"Acres" Bogs Down Despite Grand Cast', review, *San Francisco Chronicle*, 15 September, 1997.

away from the violence of the male-centred approaches embodied in the western or the gangster genres which focus on Lear's experience. Jones' screenplay (and initially Smiley's novel) presents us with both a reoriented and a remotivated narrative,[169] aligning us with Ginny's/Goneril's point of view and redefining her motivation and that of her sister, Rose/Regan, who are constructed here as sexually abused offspring. However, the screenplay's diminishment of both the novel's monetary aspects and the play's subplot, and the omission of Ginny's attempt to poison Rose reposition the narrative, remodelling it as 'a movie about sisters rather than a movie about siblings' according to Smiley. She claims Ginny's closing remark – 'I want to give the children something I never had, which is hope' – casts her in the role of 'perrenial victim': hope here is based on 'wishing and escape rather than on understanding and coming to terms'.[170] By denying Ginny the capacity to commit her own evil act the film, according to Smiley, denies her a means of coming to terms with evil in others, her father in particular.

Just as Nahum Tate's melodramatic stage version of *King Lear* ends on an optimistic note, the close of the film reflects the more upbeat cinematic conventions of melodrama rather than the tenuous resolutions offered either by Smiley's novel or Shakespeare's play. Smiley cites other instances in which novel and film treat the narrative differently, the former integrating and examining issues related to incest at an ideological level throughout while the latter uses it as a 'punchline'[171] at a much later point in its narrative

---

[169] Definitions from Douglas Lanier, *Shakespeare and Modern Popular Culture* (Oxford: Oxford University Press, 2002), p. 83.

[170] Faye P. Whitaker and Susan Carlson, 'Play to Novel to Film: an Interview with Jane Smiley on Rewriting Shakespeare', *Flyway* 5:1/2 (1999), pp.160–161.

[171] Ibid., p. 162.

structure. Whilst Smiley's novel is about the dynamics between female and male characters, the film is seen to be dominated by its women 'to the exclusion of anyone else'.[172] The film's handling of the division of the land scene is a further notable failure in the novelist's estimation: it is devoid of the necessary menace and impending doom, taking place in the sunny confines of the communal gathering held in honour of Jess's/Edmund's return and presided over by a calm and rational Larry Cook/Lear as opposed to the drunken, impulsive father drawn in the novel.[173] However, Smiley also concedes that each writer, whether of stage play, novel or screenplay, 'uses the tools of its genre to gain and communicate insight into the material', and that its continued recycling is a 'testament' to the 'ongoing power' of the Lear myth as a narrative template.[174] As such, what Smiley sees as fundamental flaws in the film may be construed as conscious inclusions and omissions related to the governing codes and conventions of on-screen melodrama, written for a cinema-going audience in a post-feminist era.

Both novel and film operate beyond the confines of tragedic conventions; they deal instead with the conventions of domestic fiction, relating a 'representative story, not an extreme story'[175] in a realistic manner. Tragic notions of the hero of Western tragedy and Western literature, and Western philosophical positions about the significance of that hero's demise, are consciously abandoned in pursuit of a more credible and sustainable depiction of life. Similarly, despite the novel being commandeered as a feminist text, there is little to suggest that Ginny or Rose, late seventies Iowa housewives

---

[172] Ibid., p. 162.
[173] Ibid., p. 162.
[174] Ibid., p. 166.
[175] Ibid., p. 153.

whose community is dominated by a male work ethos and female domesticity, see themselves as feminists or as part of that whole debate. They are constructed in novel and film as unwittingly repressed individuals, similar to the various heroines found in the fifties melodramas of Douglas Sirk, operating within a strictly delineated domestic space as part of a stable society with a strong moral code.

The novel examines issues at a personal level; however, like Shakespeare's play, it also presents us with a critique of patriarchy, in this instance through its contextualising of the political via an exploration of the monetary fall-out of Larry's division of the land and its critique of capitalism in general. The film is much more concerned with the personal issues being confronted by the sisters – including their own material transgressions as well as those of their father – than with any of the wider implications of a failed patriarchal system. Yet the film's focus on the personal does not necessarily make it a lesser text. Its engagement with feminist issues is there by inference, even though cloaked in the more palatable populist guise of the familiar codes and conventions of the melodrama: the emotional life of women is foregrounded and given a voice through which the problems associated with social constructs of femininity and male exploitation of women are addressed.

But given the conventions of melodrama in particular and its classification as a genre of integration/indeterminate space in general, the extent of any such critique is inevitably limited. According to Barry Langford, melodrama belongs to a 'fundamentally non-contestatory mode, one that insists on the rightness and the validity of binding social institutions such as marriage and family'.[176] Like the musical or the romantic comedy, it occupies an

[176] Langford, p. 37.

ideological space characterised by its stability and is dependent upon 'a highly conventionalised value system'.[177] The community's values are not challenged directly – the abuses perpetrated by the grand patriarch, Larry Cook, are never revealed to the community at large, despite Rose's deathbed wishes – and the stable milieu provided by that community is sustained. It remains an ideologically stable and civilised space because the transgressions of the community's father figure are kept hidden.

The protagonist's struggle to align, or realign, her views with those of the community at large forms the stock narrative force for such dramas. Yet within family melodramas there surface 'contradictory imperatives' battling to both expose and repress the flaws within the family unit,[178] and it is Ginny's inner struggle in coming to terms with her repressed memories of paternal sexual abuse that forms this film's ideological and narrative focus. Our viewing experience is filtered through Ginny's voice-over, giving us intimate access to her psychological conflict and narrating events from her perspective: we identify here with the female position rather than aligning our sympathies with the ageing Lear figure, Larry Cook. However, conventionally, while the genre of integration foregrounds female experience, it engages more often with the experience of the feminised couple/group, and in *A Thousand Acres*, even though Ginny's story dominates, it is Ginny and Rose, presented as the wronged couple, whose path we follow. They share the secret of their abuse and of their adulterous affairs with Jess. There are numerous moments in which the sisters share the cinematic frame in shot compositions dominated by scenes in kitchens, on the porches of their homes, on the perimeters of their

---

[177] Schatz in Braudy and Cohen. Oxford University Press: 2004, p. 698.
[178] Langford, p. 47.

gardens, looking out onto fields populated by labouring men and machinery who are constructed in binary opposition to the sisters' domesticated domain. We are also presented with stock melo-dramatic deathbed moments complete with trite, sentimental dialogue; Ginny's line, 'What am I going to do without you', cuts to the prescribed close-up of their tightly held hands, as Rose delivers her final summation: 'I don't have any accomplishments … I didn't get Daddy to know what he did. But I saw without being afraid, without turning away. I didn't forgive the unforgivable'. Ginny's voice-over is similarly loaded with emotive excess, her assumption that they would 'always be together, forever on this thousand acres', or that 'the hardest part was leaving Rose', underlining the sisterly bond at the core of this tale.

However, the contradictory imperatives at work within *A Thousand Acres* make for a closure that breaks away from the expected reintegration of the protagonists into the communal fold. Both Ginny and Rose are seen as pillars of their conformist Iowa farming community through their affiliation with the Cook dynasty. Their identities are firmly rooted in their position as daughters of the community's leading patriarch. Rose wants to shatter the smug morality of the community that reveres a man who she knows is an incestuous bully and it is her dying wish that Ginny expose him; yet she has never chosen either to expose him during her lifetime or to leave that community, even though she sends her daughters into a safer environment. Ginny, on the other hand, chooses to leave, rejecting the community and its values at a personal level and forging for herself a different kind of identity, but she refuses to confront the immorality fostered within its midst. In line with the conventions of melodrama as a film genre, the status quo is maintained at a societal level, and the female voice, though found, is then silenced.

But the choice, as in all melodrama, ultimately lies with the female protagonist. Moreover, at a personal level, Ginny seems to have resolved her inner conflicts; she has come to terms with the repressed memories of her abuse. Yet, unlike the heroines of forties and fifties melodramas, she subverts generic expectation by choosing to leave home, husband and community, relinquishing – and thus critiquing in the process – all of the familial values for which they stand. Although Smiley may regard Ginny's film persona as the perennial victim, within the parameters of the melodrama genre, Ginny's choice may be defined as heroic. The progression from 'romantic antagonism' to 'eventual embrace', outlined as central to the genres of integration,[179] revolves in this instance around the repressed memories that Ginny eventually learns to embrace: she deals with them and moves on, refusing to become the victim of the status quo. The embrace envisaged in Shakespeare's play, in which Lear is reconciled with Cordelia and with his own short-comings, does not materialise in this film text, though screen time is devoted to a moment when Larry and Caroline/Cordelia are overheard reminiscing over a misplaced memory, Larry's reference to Caroline as the 'little birdie girl' echoing Lear's sentiment in the play's reunion scene. However, here the embrace between Larry and Caroline is used as a plot device, triggering Ginny's repressed memory of sexual abuse and realised on screen as a flashback, enabling her to finally acknowledge her past.

As a dynastic melodrama *A Thousand Acres* bears striking similarities to Sirk's *Written on the Wind* (1956), a melodrama which, according to Langford, 'associates issues of patriarchal authority in decline with eruptions of sexual and social deviance, and further links these pathologies to business and industrial crises', the collapse

---

[179] Schatz, p. 698.

of one being 'directly implicated in the breakdown of the other'.[180] The breakdown within the domestic arena in *A Thousand Acres* is precipitated by Larry's division of the land, an act soon regretted by this petulant patriarch, linking his domestic pathologies to his self-induced business/industrial crisis. When Larry first appears on screen he dominates the frame in a low-angle shot, Ginny standing subserviently in the background. His privileged place within the community is established at the film's outset as they gather to celebrate the return of Harold Clarke's prodigal son, Jess. We are presented with a tableau of communal harmony, all picnic tables and home-baked fare; Ginny and Rose are very much a part of its ethos as they arrive with their own pies and pastries. We enter knowingly into the domestic sphere heralded by the film's genre, and the voice-over saturation that sets the story in motion leaves us in no doubt as to its engagement with female experience, despite our intertextual assumptions about the direction a narrative based on the *Lear* myth will take. Even the division of the land scene, denounced as bland and ineffectual by Smiley, is reconfigured in line with the motivations of the melodrama genre. It is a moment that traditionally revolves around the Lear figure, his personality dominating the scene, but in *A Thousand Acres* the division is conducted in an almost casual, conversational manner at the celebratory picnic. It is a moment which is devoid of emotive energy, focusing audience attention not on male experience but on female responses to male actions, and it subverts our expectations – expectations which are intrinsically linked to Shakespeare's version of events.

Jess's role is also redefined according to the female driven conventions of melodrama. No longer the charismatic anti-hero,

[180] Langford, p. 48.

he becomes the transient representative of a new order, a new value system that operates outside the set values of the land-bound community so central to *A Thousand Acres*. He is the catalyst for the sisters' adulterous transgressions, providing the impetus for the stock temptation at the core of melodrama. However, unlike the heroines of forties and fifties melodramas like *Brief Encounter* (1945) and *All That Heaven Allows* (1955), the transgressions of Ginny and Rose are realised, providing a turning point for the formerly submissive Ginny. In true melodramatic style, her unruly desires erupt first in the domestic sphere in the form of an adulterous affair but, more importantly, they lead her to question the wider social order and her father's prominent place within it.

The excessive visual style of fifties melodrama is cited by feminist theorists as a 'subversion of ideological norms'.[181] Unable to transgress in reality, the unruly desires of the fifties heroine of melodrama are realised instead through the creation of a coded *mise en scène*, evoked by a lush, seductive colour palette characterised by visual excess, and providing a 'cathartic burst of cinematic rapture for the audience to counterpoint the joy denied the heroine'.[182] In *A Thousand Acres* Moorhouse's focus on the beauty and the grandeur of the land creates a similar visual excess: shots of vast stretches of fertile land coloured by autumnal sunshine establish an overwhelming sense of place not only in the film's opening moments but throughout. Such shots establish Ginny's connection with the land her family has farmed for generations, acting as visual shorthand for the immense hold it has over her, and explaining in part her continued presence in what we come to know is a place imbibed with memories of childhood abuse. The storm scene offers

[181] Ibid., p. 30.

[182] Richard Falcon, 'Magnificent Obsession', *Sight and Sound* 13.3 (2003), p. 14.

a visual contrast to such colour-drenched landscape shots; grey clouds, thunder, lightning, accompanied by a highly dramatic orchestral score provide the backdrop to Larry's vitriolic and unprovoked verbal attack on Ginny and Rose, the *mise en scène* reflecting the ugliness of his lines as he labels Ginny a 'dried up bitch' and threatens to 'throw you whores off this place'. Rose's similarly unprovoked rage erupts during a moment of seeming domestic harmony as the family gathers to play Monopoly, suggesting undercurrents of emotion not yet expressed. Such emotive excess is also characteristic of the genre's performance style: it is a mode that is heavily dependent upon acting styles and upon quality of performance. The deathbed scenes, punctuated by the kind of excessive orchestral score associated with melodrama and loaded with emotive dialogue, could become mawkish and trite, but the measured performances of Jessica Lange and Michelle Pfeiffer lend the scenes a credibility and poignancy that belies the genre's inherent sentimentality. Without such performances 'women's weepies', rescued for critical attention by seventies feminists, could easily regress to being regarded as a 'despised form', wallowing in sentiment rather than 'offer(ing) objects of study to which women's experience (is) central'.[183]

By placing the narrative within the realms of melodrama Jones shifts the focus not only to female experience but to small-town repression and preoccupations of the personal rather than the universal. For some critics this detracts from the major issues addressed in its literary forerunners.[184] Such criticism highlights some of the problems faced by the screenwriter whose aim is to employ

[183] Falcon, p. 12.
[184] Roger Ebert, 'A Thousand Acres', review, *Chicago Sun-Times*, 19 September, 1997.

a populist genre format to the adaptation of any iconic literary text; the problem is exacerbated in this instance by the fact that Jones is dealing with the reworking of both a classic, modernist novel and, by intertextual reference, a classic Renaissance play. When reconfigured in the guise of melodrama, these problems are compounded by the fact that we are now in a post-feminist era in which the credibility of the 'heroic' female victim is far less sustainable.

King Lear goes art house: acts of reconstruction

Inventive art house offshoots of *King Lear* can present us with cinematic interpretations that, like Peter Brook's canonical *Lear*, imbibe the ideological concerns found in Shakespeare's text in a way that differs considerably from existing mainstream genre reconfigurations of the play, and can explore facets of the text that would remain buried within the spectacle of a more conservative, fidelity-driven heritage rendition. Steve Rumbelow's *King Lear* (1976), French New Wave auteur Jean-Luc Godard's *King Lear* (1987), and Dogme 'brother' Kristian Levring's *The King Is Alive* (2000) operate beyond the realms of mainstream genre cinema; they are stylistically experimental, with accepted film practice and narrative expectations being outlawed to varying degrees. However, not all of these *avant garde* takes on Shakespeare's *King Lear* are cinematic successes of the same calibre as Brook's experimental adaptation.

The art film replaces story with 'authorial expressivity', a 'drifting episodic' treatment of narrative time and space, and 'psychologically complex characters' whose conflicts are internalised.[185] Its

---

[185] David Bordwell, 'The Art of Cinema as a Mode of Film Practice', *Film Criticism* 4.1 (1979), pp. 57–58.

art house author/filmmaker becomes a central unifying force within the structure of such films, his style signature an expected convention within the narrative, his means of telling the tale as important – if not more so – than the story he relates. Whereas Shakespeare's narratives are of classic story design, the art house film works in opposition to that narrative mode, standing against the kind of cause and effect momentum once seen as central to mainstream genre cinema. All of the art house treatments of *King Lear* use it as inspiration, as one of a number of intertexts at play in the film's creation, and work towards a purposeful deconstruction and subsequent reconstruction of elements of the appropriated *Lear* text. These renditions of *King Lear* also share with Brook's 1971 film a leaning towards the absurd, and echo the existential angst found in Beckett's *Waiting for Godot* and *Endgame*.

Rumbelow's *King Lear* is informed by the theatrical methods of Antonin Artaud: it is an intellectually challenging deconstruction and subsequent reconstruction of the *Lear* narrative in which the director purposely mirrors the act of reconstruction undertaken in relation to what we now view as Shakespeare's version of *King Lear*, the Quarto and Folio editions of which are themselves 'remembered' reconstructions of an Ur-text. Similarly, Godard's post-apocalyptic setting provides the backdrop for protagonist William Shakespeare Junior's search for the lost texts of his ancestor, and what narrative momentum is established revolves around his futile quest to reconstruct these texts from lines that have survived in the collective memory in some form, no matter how distorted or disjointed. Levring is also engaging in these acts of *construction* in *The King Is Alive*, though reconstruction of the Shakespearean text takes on a more literal dimension within this film's narrative, its stranded travellers seeking to perform the play and finding themselves in the lines they reconstruct in the process.

Made on a shoe-string budget provided by a British Film Institute grant, Rumbelow's *King Lear*, with a running time of just forty-five minutes, is as far from the realms of mainstream cinema as is cinematically possible. The film is an intellectually challenging and intriguing piece of *performative* innovation, but this *King Lear*, which has its roots in the Triple Action Theatre Group's absurdist stage version of the play, does not translate successfully to the screen: its indebtedness to its own theatrical origins[186] and to Shakespeare's original presents an insurmountable obstacle to its relocation to the medium of film. Rumbelow continues to work within the temporal and spatial constraints of the stage rather than the screen, emphasising abstract elements and sculpting the language of Shakespeare's play into a kind of visual physicality. Rooted as it is in theatrical practice rather than cinematic practice, it is a film that has no real place in a film industry context. It is an adaptation that is less 'quantum leap',[187] more Dada-esque reinvention, emerging as a cross between art house cinema and filmed theatre and, whilst interesting from a performative per-spective, should be regarded as a filmed essay rather than as a commercially viable film product. As such it has limited relevance to the study of *cinematic* Shakespeares.

'Meantime we shall express our darker purpose' – Jean-Luc Godard's King Lear (1987)

Like Rumbelow, Godard trades on the cultural associations afforded by appropriation of the title *King Lear* and uses it as a starting point for a discourse on the failings of patriarchy and the

---

[186] Rumbelow's *Triple Action Theatre Group* first performed this absurdist stage version of *King Lear* in 1975.

[187] Marowitz, p. 15.

fragmentary, meaningless nature of existence. His storyline involves retired mafia boss, Don Learo, and his daughter; however, the film's limited narrative momentum revolves instead around Shakespeare's fictitious descendant, William Shakespeare Junior, and his attempts to reconstruct and record his famous ancestor's lost narratives within this post-apocalyptic world. As with Rumbelow's *King Lear*, this cinematic offshoot borders the realms of filmed essay: its director's meditations on the relationship between image and word, film-maker and film financier take precedence over the kind of anticipated narrative cogency of mainstream cinematic practice. Even though Godard is operating within the conventions of experimental art house cinema, he pushes the boundaries of what constitutes cinematic experience in his *King Lear*.

Godard chooses to retain the title of the original text as a cultural referent, bringing with it all of its associated ideologies and high art affiliations. However, whilst Rumbelow's film is trapped in a co-dependent relationship with both the Shakespearean play and the Triple Action Theatre Group's former stage production, Godard's text – as with Brook's film text – exists beyond the confines of the appropriated stage play and operates firmly within the realms of art house cinema, creating what Susan Bennett terms a 'proactive relation to the Ur-texts of culture'.[188] He seeks to deconstruct the Lear myth in much the same way as he deconstructs the Carmen myth in his *Prenom: Carmen* (1983), dislocating our preconceived notions of each and forcing us to a realisation that there is no fixed locus of meaning in any given text, regardless of its seemingly untouchable cultural status. But whilst an audience's detailed knowledge of Shakespeare's play is not a prerequisite for meaning-

---

[188] Susan Bennett, 'Godard and *Lear*: Trashing the Can(n)on', *Theatre Survey* 39:1, (1998), p. 12.

ful engagement with Godard's film, familiarity with the play's preoccupations aids understanding. It is part of his signature style to introduce layers of intertextual referencing within his films, and in his *King Lear* (1987) Shakespeare's text is supplemented by the inclusion of a vast range of works of art, from the paintings of Velazquez, Botticelli, Renoir and Goya, to photographs of various fathers of the world of cinema, to visual and verbal allusions to Shakespeare's Sonnets 47 and 60, Robert Bresson's *Joan of Arc*, and Virginia Woolf's *The Waves*. The film exhibits a lack of narrative cohesion and a seeming irreverence not only for genre and industry expectations but for Shakespeare's text. Godard's darker purpose has less to do with Shakespeare than with his intent to present an intellectual puzzle which parodies the commercial film industry and interrogates all facets of patriarchal power. He employs alienation techniques engineered to distance the audience and to ensure its active engagement with the *ideas* explored within his film rather than with characters or any form of narrative momentum, presenting us instead with firstly a meditation upon patriarchal power in its many guises, and secondly philosophical musings on the relationship between words and visual images. He is, according to Susan Bennett, more interested in 'the business of *how* a text, especially one as culturally protected as *King Lear*, can be made to *mean* – for whom and to what ends and, most of all, at what cost', rather than in 'the business of interpreting text'.[189]

Initially Godard was to direct the film using a screenplay written by and starring novelist Norman Mailer as the story's mafiosa Lear figure but on-set disagreements swiftly resulted in Mailer's departure. From a genre perspective, Godard's *King Lear* purports to be both gangster and sci-fi film, yet in reality it refuses to conform

[189] Ibid., p. 14.

to the generic conventions and expectations of either on all but the most rudimentary level. Despite his longstanding interest in the Hollywood gangster, first explored in *À Bout de Souffle* (1960), the gangster connections in Godard's *King Lear* are extremely limited. Neither the plot lines nor the iconographic expectations of the gangster genre are realised in this film. Lear and his entourage are referred to as Don Learo, Don Gloucester, Don Kenny and so on paying lip service to the gangster genre; Mailer's opening scene, shot before his dramatic departure and retained in the film's final cut, also makes verbal reference to the gangster genre, his character claiming that 'the Mafia is the only way to do Lear'; and at one point Cordelia types the dictated words of her father, retired Mafia boss Don Learo, as he constructs his book about American gangsters but these are mere nods to the genre as are a number of restaurant scenes that echo, at an iconographic level, the stock moments in the gangster film in which business is conducted over food either in the public domain of the restaurant or within the more private confines of the family dining room. And although Don Learo employs a suitably gangsteresque inflection in his delivery, he does not emerge as the gangster genre's male hero whose quest shapes the narrative. The physical absence of any mob associates further undermines his credibilty as retired mobster.

If any quest emerges at all it is that of William Shakespeare Junior who seeks to reconstruct his ancestor's lost texts: Don Learo serves only as an example of the gangster genre's association with failed patriarchal power. Similarly, whilst supposedly set in a post-apocalyptic world and billed as a science fiction film, there are no visible signs of post-Chernobyl destruction and any references to this being a futuristic scenario come via exceedingly dry moments of exposition in which Shakespeare Junior tells us of the present situation and of the destruction of works of art resulting from the disaster with lines such as 'Chernobyl, and everything disappears'. Images of a Chernobyl-fuelled apocalypse do not materialise, despite Godard's later musings on the power of the visual image.

Godard emphasises production issues from the outset: the first reference to his financiers, the Cannon Group, comes in the opening moments in the form of a taped telephone conversation, played in voice-over, between Godard and a Cannon executive who is pressing the director for a finished product. Voice-over and accompanying on-screen images are totally unconnected, presenting a disjointed and fragmented relationship that, although of little apparent relevance to narrative momentum, reflects the lack of harmony between film-maker and film financier. The garbled nature of the voice-over contrasts with the unhurried, lingering shots of the art work passing before the eye of the camera. Godard also uses the opening frames to attack Mailer via a directorial voice-over which labels him 'The Great Writer' who engages in 'a Ceremony of Star Behaviour', again highlighting Godard's distaste of all things Hollywood and his concern with exploring matters unrelated to traditional storytelling.

Godard returns to this preoccupation with Hollywood through-out the film, demonising the commercial film industry via his commentary on the financial, power-hungry corporations repre-sented here by his financial backers, Cannon Films. In role as the bizarre Professor Pluggy, Godard argues that 'when we lose money we lose nothing' but 'when we lose character we lose everything', implying that to sell out to the corporations is to prostitute oneself to the commercial film industry. It seems that Godard's main aim in this film is to exact an artistic revenge on his backers by presenting them with an incoherent, unmarketable product, exploring in the process the near impossibility of making films. Shakespeare Junior's quest to recapture the lost works of his ancestor is financed by

Cannon as a corporate investment, demonstrating once more the ways in which, according to Godard, art – his own included – can be hijacked by the corporation. At one point in the film, France and Burgundy are replaced by corporate film financiers DWA and Fox as barterers for Cordelia's love; Shakespeare's verse merges with Godard's commentary about Cannon as Don Learo asks Cordelia, 'My joy, to whose young loves DWA and Twentieth Century Fox shine to be of interest, what can you say?' Pluggy consistently refers to a Mr Alien who we surmise is representative of the Cannon Group (realised on-screen by Woody Allen, seen briefly editing the film in the closing frames) and who at the end of the film is in charge. In voice-over, Shakespeare Junior tells us that:

> The bad times of Chernobyl had been long forgotten. Paramount, Fox, Warners were booming. I was finishing the picture, or bringing this twisted fairy tale to an end. The man in charge was named Mr Alien. This can be no accident.

The closing remark is intentionally cryptic, leaving us to ponder what Godard may mean, but there remains a disconcerting edge of Godardian paranoia embedded in his parodic treatment of the commercial film industry.

Just as Rumbelow's *King Lear* is more 'critical essay written with a camera'[190] than effective narrative cinema, Godard's *King Lear* is, according to David Impastato, first and foremost 'a film of ideas, of criticism', and one which 'ignor(es) the implications of the market place'.[191] As *avant garde* films which adopt an anti-genre stance

[190] Sinyard in *Filming Literature: The Art of Screen Adaptation*, p. 23.

[191] David Impastato, 'Godard's *Lear*: Why is it so Bad?', *Shakespeare Bulletin* 12:3 (1994), p. 38.

they cannot, however, escape some form of generic classification, whether as the conventionally unconventional art house film[192] or as part of an emerging genre of filmed essays with their own set of conventions and fragmented narrative patterns. Whatever the motivations are behind this film – and narrative clarity is not one of them – Godard's appropriation of Shakespeare's *King Lear* is at best selective, but there are numerous tentative links forged between play and screenplay despite his irreverent treatment of the text. Jessica Maerz's contention that it is a film which is more concerned with its own history and conditions of production than with the play text seems well-founded given Godard's constant foregrounding of issues related to the relationship between himself and Cannon;[193] however, his 'meditations' also interrogate the relationship between image and sound, verbal and linguistic signifiers as effective means of communication in the world of the cinema, and there are clearly moments when screenplay and playscript connect. In voice-over, Godard claims 'Words are reckless ... Words are one thing and reality is another thing ... There is "no thing"', suggesting, as does the Shakespearean text in its emphasis upon the word 'Nothing', that language is an unreliable, unstable signifier. Furthermore, in role as Professor Pluggy, he asks Shakespeare Junior, 'What are you writing for?' claiming that 'When nobody writes the writing still exists', and thus posing further questions about the nature and significance of the Ur-texts of our culture. Junior's response compounds the issue: for him the problem is obvious – 'No names, no lines, no story.'

[192] Robert McKee, *Story: Substance, Structure, Style and the Principles of Screenwriting* (London: Methuen, 1999), p. 88.

[193] Jessica Maerz, 'Godard's *King Lear*: Referents Provided Upon Request', *Literature/ Film Quarterly* 32.2 (2004), p. 113.

In this context, Godard's refusal to engage in coherent narrative forms and clearly delineated characters has a philosophical justification, although as an audience we surely tend to agree with Shakespeare Junior who decries the lack of plot lines and character motivations, both of which are successfully explicated by the words of the Shakespearean source text Godard's Junior seeks to rediscover. Instead, it is the image which is, according to Professor Pluggy, 'a pure creation of the soul … a reconciliation of two realities', capable of an emotive power in direct proportion to its capacity to distance itself from the audience. However, his ruminations overlay a set of images of plastic dinosaur models glaringly lit by a naked light bulb: said images lack context, have no connection to any narrative thread within the film text, and fail to evoke an emotional response from his viewers. Perhaps the anticipated emotion is one of audience frustration, again in line with Godard's overall parodic intent; the debate about the role of images continues in a scene involving an interview with a New York journalist who listens intently to Pluggy's incoherent ramblings, suggesting that Godard is mocking the whole media coverage of cinematic issues.

Images of artists and their fathers, and of 'fathers' of the cinema like Orson Welles, are projected in a sequence of black and white stills which seem totally unrelated to the two overlapping voice-overs, one of which continues the debate about the significance of the image, though the exact nature of either discourse is lost amidst a cacophony of sounds, from the background noises of the restaurant to the winds roaring around the sea shore. This distancing of the audience as a means of ensuring their intellectual engagement is part of Godard's counter-cinematic style, but whereas in his earlier films there is at least a narrative established before it is interrupted by such techniques, in Godard's *King Lear* narrative intransitivity is a constant: the narrative is not broken or interrupted because it is never established. However, there are moments in this sequence which successfully remind us of the *thematic* connections between Godard's images and Shakespeare's *King Lear*. Peter Donaldson's in-depth study of the patriarchal relationships explored in Godard's film details the many ways in which it 'appropriates the riches of (Shakespeare's) paternal text'; Godard presents us with what Donaldson terms 'a distanced and debased model' of the Shakespearean text but one which 'sometimes establishes sudden intimate connection to its parent while dissembling its filial relationship'.[194] The connections of father to child, artist to disciples, artist to his own creations, film-financier to filmmaker, source text to adaptation are all explored by Godard during the course of the film, creating 'a metaphoric, free-associative play on the theme of fatherhood'[195] which is much more reflective of the concerns anchored in Shakespeare's play than are meditations upon the power of the image itself.

Godard points out at the start of the film that, 'It was not Lear with three daughters. It was Kate with three fathers: Mailer the star, Mailer as father and me as director – too much indeed'. His observations bring to the fore the issues shared by both play script and screenplay: patriarchal control, its ultimate demise and its systematic abuse of women are at the core of each, though whilst the issues are enacted via a classic story design and subtle character development in Shakespeare's play, they are *interrogated* by the interplay of image, sound and language in Godard's film, narrative momentum and clearly delineated characterisations

---

[194] Peter Donaldson, *Shakespearean Films/Shakespearean Directors* (Massachusetts: Unwin Hyman, 1990), pp. 189–190.
[195] Ibid., p. 192.

being almost non-existent. Images of artistic fathers are replaced by images of evil fathers such as Goya's *Chronos Devouring his Child*.[196] Mailer's star behaviour and swift departure presents us with a Lear-like display of petulance and power, whilst Don Learo's overly protective relationship with Cordelia smacks of the incestuous undertones subliminally located in Shakespeare's play. His response to the attentions of Shakespeare Junior – 'Are you trying to make a play for my girl? Get your hands off her' – and the bloodied sheets found in the hotel room he appears to share with Cordelia compound our suspicions. Cordelia's role remains that of carer; Ringwald is constructed as artistic prop, seen typing the words of her father and ministering to his needs yet retaining an emotional distance.

Donaldson notes that Godard works to expose male exploitation of women by demonstrating how very dependent male culture is upon female subordination.[197] And it is inferred in the film text that Godard's Don Learo shoots Cordelia, displaying the ultimate control over the female body. But Shakespeare's paternalistic text is superseded at the film's close by Virginia Woolf's novel *The Waves* which, unlike Shakespeare's play, survives intact. Despite the supposed destruction of all works of art, this female text prevails and attempts to silence the female voice fail as we cut from a shot of Don Learo sitting in front of the dead Cordelia to a shot of a young woman reading from a printed copy of *The Waves*, despite earlier indications that no printed texts have survived. Godard also shares some of the paternalistic lines from the Shakespearean text

[196] Francisco Goya's *Chronos Devouring his Child* (1823) depicts Chronos, father of Zeus, devouring one of his offspring in an attempt to avert his own downfall; having been told that he would be overthrown by one of his own sons (just as he had overthrown his father), Chronos vowed to eat all of them at their birth.

[197] Donaldson, p. 219.

with a female voice-over, challenging and renegotiating the power-play. Maerz may claim rather simplistically that Godard's film works via two distinct binary oppositions of power and virtue, Don Learo being representative of the former and Cordelia of the latter,[198] but despite her physical death, and with it the death of virtue, at the end of the film, the power rests with Cordelia at a more metaphysical level. In addition to this, Godard aligns his virtuous Cordelia with the powerful figure of Joan of Arc; as we see her dressed in virginal white and leading a white horse across an open field, a female voice-over recites lines from Bresson's *Joan of Arc*: 'It is death against whom I ride ... Against you I fling myself unvanquished and unyielding, O death!', suggesting again that even in death power is vested in her rather than the patriarchal Lear.

And yet, it remains a frustrating film to engage with due to Godard's decision to work with the text in such an abstract manner. Kenneth Rothwell may revel in it as a 'segmented and disjointed celebration of apocalypse', lauding it as a veritable 'academic feast',[199] but at the level of narrative the film is a distinct failure. Godard refuses to engage with the expectations of narrative cinema, challenging what we have come to define as cinema (within the independent or the mainstream sector) but what he offers in place of narrative cohesion is a muddled meditation on the art of constructing meaning, whether from an Ur-text or from the recesses of his own mind. The mainstay of the only clearly identifiable story line involves Shakespeare Junior's search for and reinvention of his ancestor's lost plays, pitted against a backdrop of

[198] Maerz, pp. 109–110.

[199] Kenneth Rothwell, *A History of Shakespeare on Screen* (Cambridge: Cambridge University Press, 1999), pp. 212–213.

a search for all lost art in this post-Chernobyl, post-apocalyptic setting. Shakespeare's classic story design is deconstructed before the eye of the camera and is replaced by the same kind of inconsistent, non-linear anti-structure which shapes Rumbelow's appropriation of the *Lear* myth. Lines are delivered randomly, repeated erratically and spoken by an array of disembodied off-screen voice-overs as well as by Godard's on-screen realisations of Don Learo and Cordelia. For example, the line 'Am I in France?' uttered by King Lear in the latter stages of the play are delivered by a disembodied male voice-over in the film's early stages. The reply, 'In your own kingdom, Sir' is barely audible since it is rendered redundant by the overwhelming sounds of waves and gulls. Later, given the identity and the quest of the young man seen gazing out to sea as these lines are spoken, we are able to make sense of the randomness of their delivery but they fail to provide a *clear* way into the narrative, especially for viewers who are not familiar with Shakespeare's text. The next collection of discernible lines from the play is repeated several times: we pan totally unconnected stills of art works and photographic portraits as the lines 'Come not between the dragon and his wrath' (1.1: 123) are delivered once more in a disembodied voice-over, displacing accepted cinematic structures of both visual and aural montage. There appears to be no rationale behind this repetition of the Shakespearean lines. Even when delivered on-screen by Cordelia and Don Learo, Shakespeare's lines fail to connect because they lack a context within this post-Chernobyl world. The archaic phrasing ensures that they *sound* misplaced, and at the level of narrative cause and effect they invariably *are* misplaced.

Maerz argues that Godard is more preoccupied with 'enact(ing) deconstruction' than with wholesale appropriation of Shakespeare's text; its main function, she claims, is to illustrate 'absence'

– of Godard's backers, of Mailer, of art works, of 'conventional Shakespearean representation' – which in itself forms the 'primary organising principle' of the film.[200] Perhaps the lack of narrative cogency and of expected patterns of film practice should also be read as a purposeful absence. These absences which Maerz sees as being of primary concern to Godard are, however, systematically challenged by Godard's Shakespeare Junior who is constantly at pains to create meaning and to articulate the absences. We also focus upon the act of textual creation in two other instances: in the opening frames we see Mailer in the act of construction, typing his screenplay and chuckling to himself as he says 'Oh yes, good way to begin', and this act of narrative construction is repeated as Burgess Meredith's Don Learo dictates his text to Cordelia. Throughout the film Junior searches for lost narratives, lost lines, lost characters, lost titles, at one point voicing his frustrations when unable to recall the title of Shakespeare's *As you Like It*. In addition to his arguments with Professor Pluggy about the importance of names, lines and stories, he claims in the later stages of the film to have reclaimed the lines and the plot, but acknowledges his incapacity to control the characters thereby created:

> I've reinvented the lines. I've reinvented the plot. Now it's up to the characters. Which is Dr Jeckyll and which is Mr Hyde? All I know is I can't control either of them.

Junior's ruminations suggest that the characters have an independent existence beyond that encompassed by any kind of written representation, and again asks us to take up a more proactive position in relation to the Ur-texts of Western culture.

[200] Maerz, pp. 109–100.

Godard's film presents us with a Cordelia and a Lear whose story leads Shakespeare Junior to the lost *Lear* narrative – 'Something was going on between this old man and this girl. I decided to concentrate on their story' – but their position as reinvented constructs from an earlier text does not *impose* a narrative upon them. Junior is one step behind them, constantly seen recording their words in his notebook and playing their lines to himself over and over. In one of the closing scenes, Junior and Don Learo share an intimate moment in which they work through the lost lines of the play, Junior's notebook being passed between them as a prompt whilst they actively construct the missing pieces of the text. Junior serves as the kind of pseudo 'prompter-conductor' identified by Tiffany Stern[201] as a crucial component of the Elizabethan theatre, coaxing lines from actors, and in this filmic instance from the collective pre-Chernobyl memory. Again parallels may be drawn between the practice of remembering and recording the texts of Shakespeare's plays in their Quarto and Folio formats and Junior's act of remembering and recording the remnants thereof in a post-Chernobyl world.

Furthermore, during a particularly bizarre woodland scene, we see a random collection of Pluggy's disciples following behind Shakespeare Junior, mimicking his every movement in what may be seen as a visual re-enactment of the adaptation process itself: the moves/words/thought processes of another are being re-formed and reshaped before the camera, the results of which may lead to the creation of a Jeckyll or a Hyde with an independent will. David Impastato argues that Godard is constantly questioning the role of the author in this film. He claims that the apparent

---

[201] Tiffany Stern, *Rehearsal from Shakespeare to Sheridan* (Oxford: Clarendon Press, 2000), p. 12.

murder of Professor Pluggy and of Shakespeare Junior 'can be viewed in the light of Roland Barthes' *The Death of the Author*, the author being 'merely a subject position in an infinite web of discourses', with Godard himself as self-sacrificing author who 'honours the multivalence and ambiguity of artistic creation'.[202] Godard openly admits his films are also criticism,[203] and in his *King Lear* he demonstrates how problematic the notion of authorial integrity and intent can be, inferring that there can be no stable nucleus of meaning even within a text of established cultural status. He employs cinematic alienation in an effort to ensure audience engagement with his meditations at an intellectual rather than an emotional level, interjecting images with a vast array of inter titles and purposefully disjointed screen/sound pairings which produce a film text that possesses neither narrative momentum nor credible character constructs. As such, it remains an extremely frustrating viewing experience despite its intellectual posturing and Godard's anti-genre stance serves to alienate his audience.

[202] Impastato, p. 39.

[203] Jonathan Rosenbaum, 'Theory and Practice: The Criticism of Jean-Luc Godard', *Sight and Sound* 41.3 (1972).

'Radical art phalanx' versus 'a clever flag of PR convenience':[204] Kristian Levring's The King Is Alive (2000)

Kristian Levring's *The King is Alive* is a product of the Danish Dogme New Wave, a movement which emerged in the mid-nineties as a backlash against Hollywood's global domination of the film industry. The democratising and anarchic intent of the Dogme New Wave is outlined in its manifesto; its aim is to bring about 'the ultimate democratisation of the cinema' by envisioning a style of film-making which adheres to a strict set of rules (a 'Vow of Chastity' to which all Dogme film-makers must pledge allegiance) that outlaws artifice and expensive technologies.[205]

Whilst *The King Is Alive* uses Shakespeare as a source of inspiration, there is no attempt to reappropriate the narrative of *King Lear* in its entirety. There are, however, undeniable connections between the predicaments of characters found in Shakespeare's *Lear* and Levring's film: familial and patriarchal failure, sexual inadequacies and identity crises abound, and true to Dogme's commitment to create films which are realistic, character-driven ensembles rather than sensationalistic convention-ridden set pieces, the film takes as its focus the exploration of the psyche and the relationships of its protagonists in real time. It avoids both the kind of

[204] Jonathan Romney, 'Overruled,' review, *New Statesman*, 4 October, 1999.

[205] The *Dogme95 Manifesto*, penned by Lars Von Trier, Thomas Vinterberg, Søren Kragh Jakobsen and Kristian Levring in the Spring of 1995 sets out strict rules for production of a film: shooting must be done on location; props and sets must not be brought in; the sound must never be produced apart from the images or vice versa; the camera must be hand-held – any movement or immobility attainable in the hand is permitted; the film must be in colour; special lighting is not acceptable; optical work and filters are forbidden; the film must not contain superficial action; temporal and geographical alienation are forbidden - the film takes place here and now; genre movies are not acceptable; the film format must be Academy 35mm; the director must not be credited. Online: www.dogme95

fragmented, narrative pyrotechnics of the so-called art house film and the more fantastical elements of genre cinema, but builds to creative effect on the absurdist nature of Shakespeare's text. Liz tells her troubled husband, 'You don't have to worry. Nobody falls in love. And everybody dies in the end', momentarily echoing the nullity and existentialist angst realised in earlier cinematic appropriations of *King Lear*, from Brook's 1971 version to the eighties renditions of Kurosawa and Godard.

The King is Alive is structured, ostensibly, around the survivor narrative as a group of stranded Western travellers awaiting rescue resort to putting on a play (*King Lear*) to maintain morale. Narrative emphasis, however, lies not with their quest for physical survival and ultimate return to Westernised 'safety' but with the emotional journeying of the travellers, realised via their enactment of *King Lear*. The cast consists of a menagerie of characters who at first operate at the level of cultural stereotype: we have Jack, the rugged Australian who attempts to save the travellers, setting off into the desert wilderness to seek help; we have numerous Americans abroad ranging from the empty-headed Gina, to the embittered couple, Liz and Ray, whose problems are exacerbated by their travels, and Ashley, the token alcoholic businessman. French intellectual, Catherine, serves initially as their antithesis, whilst Henry, an ageing English actor-turned-Hollywood-script-doctor, bridges the cultural divisions within the group. We also have a troubled British family trio (domineering father Charles, dominated son/domineering husband Paul and victim wife Amanda). Outside this Westernised clan stand the beleaguered African bus driver Moses and the tale's distanced narrator, Kanana, whose chorus-like voice-over pieces together the events that make up Levring's story.

The experimental style of the Dogme New Wave bears a striking resemblance to Brook's counter-cinematic approach to the filming of *King Lear* back in the seventies: both Brook and Levring employ jump cuts, canted shots, static frames of considerable duration. And like Brook, Levring emphasises the word over and above the use of emotionally manipulative non-diegetic score, both directors attempting to return us to the blanker canvas of the Elizabethan/ Jacobean stage. Levring's choice is in part preordained by the Dogme rule which forbids the use of sound produced independent of image,[206] but his adherence to this particular edict enhances audience engagement, leaving us free to respond without the intrusive signalling of a melodramatic soundtrack.

Stripped of technology, in accordance with their manifesto's edicts, the focus of Levring's film comes back to two of the momentous forces at the heart of Shakespearean narration: character and language. The visual spectacle achieved by Levring is not earned at the expense of costly production values but through careful choice of location and conscious rejection of many facets of mainstream cinematic language, resulting in a recycled version of *King Lear* which defies conservative, heritage genre expectations. It presents us with a fragmentary take on the narrative, employing low budget strategies which are in direct opposition to the high production values of the majority of adaptations of filmed Shakespeare in its purest sense. Unlike Hollywood productions, filming takes place chronologically, ensuring a sense of narrative and performative continuity which deals in what Levring terms 'real time', the 'line between rehearsal and performance becom(ing) blurred'.[207] Temporal and geographical reality

[206] Dogme Manifesto, Rule Two: the sound must never be produced apart from images and vice-versa.

[207] Kristian Levring in interview with Peter Rundle, 'An Aesthetic Choice: excerpts from a phone interview given by Kristian Levring', 10 November, 1999.
Online: www.dogme95.dk/news/interview/levring_interview.htm

are retained in accordance with Dogme intent and the end product achieves a sense of immediacy and credibility despite its use of literary conceit, the play-within-the-play conceit being used as a vehicle for character development.

Unlike his eighties predecessor, Jean-Luc Godard, Levring creates a meaningful dialogue with Shakespeare's text without losing sight of the market place entirely and without sacrificing characterisation and narrative momentum. Levring sees *The King is Alive* as a film about 'what happens to people ... when they start thinking about who they are',[208] and their predicament as stranded travellers in a forbidding wilderness, when coupled with the film's exploration of identity, offers obvious parallels with Shakespeare's *King Lear*. According to Levring, Dogme script-writing is about a return to 'character writing', where 'the only way you can solve problems is actually by solving your characters'; it is not plot-driven in any way and there are no arbitrary plot twists nor overtly realised generic expectations.[209] However, his denial of generic conventions is arguably a ruse: it is, after all, a survival story during the course of which a means to staying alive is pursued, even if it takes the less conventional route of 'let's put on a show' to maintain group morale rather than half-hearted attempts to become hunter-gatherers.

They do engage in stock survival genre actions, several of the characters seeking to repair damaged shelters and to attract out-side attention by constructing a system of reflecting light, whilst Australian Jack sets off into the desert wilderness to find help. And yet it remains an unconventional rendition of the survival story,

---

[208] Kristian Levring in an interview with Richard Kelly, *The Name of the Book is Dogme95* (London: Thames and Hudson Ltd, 2000), p. 50.

[209] Kristian Levring in interview with Peter Chumo, 'Script Comments', *Creative Screenwriting* 8.4 (2001), p. 20.

despite the fact that we are dealing with travellers stranded in the desert. Levring's initial inspiration comes not from the narrative patterning of the survival story but from his recollection of a British friend living in the Mojave Desert just outside California who, to assuage his homesickness, would organise impromptu Shakespeare evenings: 'he('d) get Chuck, the man who runs the gas station to be Hamlet, and Liz from the diner to be Ophelia, and they('d) just sit around and read the play'.[210] Shakespeare's *King Lear* serves here as a staging device through which the characters created by Levring may find themselves: the narrative momentum of the film is shaped around the literary conceit of staging the play, echoing Shakespeare's use of a similar conceit in *Hamlet* where the play-within-a-play is designed to catch the conscience of the king. Although first drawn to *Hamlet* – a play which remains an intertextual reference point at various moments within the film's narrative – Levring's decision to explore his characters through the staging of *King Lear* instead is also conditioned by the absurdist nature of both the play and the travellers' attempts to perform it under such adverse conditions. Like the asylum inmates in Brook's absurdist *Marat/Sade* (1967), Levring's travellers put on a show as a means to psychological survival.

The film is thus invested with a certain level of theatricality that builds on previous appropriations of the *Lear* text. Peter Yates's *The Dresser* (1983) presents us with another theatrically self-conscious reworking of the *Lear* narrative, though Ronald Harwood's screenplay establishes its theatricality and its connection with Shakespeare's text at a much more literal level, especially in relation to its character types. Sir is the tyrannical lead actor/father figure of a travelling theatre company/family; questions of loyalty and betrayal within this theatrical family are written into the narrative and there are the identifiable battles between the old order –

represented by Sir, his dresser/Fool, Norman, and stage manager, Kent/Madge – and a new order, in the guise of the scheming Irene, an amalgamation of Cordelia, Regan and Goneril, and the rebellious Oxenby, a pseudo-Edmund. Sir's identity crisis also echoes that of Lear, though again the parallels are translated in a literal sense as Sir blackens his face for a performance of *Othello* when he should be playing King Lear. As in *The King Is Alive*, reality and theatrics merge: after witnessing the destruction caused by the bombs dropped in this World War II setting, Sir momentarily loses his sanity, his irrational behaviour mirroring that of the outcast Lear on the heath. The narrative here is driven by backstage dramas, focusing predominantly upon Sir's dresser, Norman, but staged scenes from *King Lear* punctuate the inevitable downfall of Sir – and by inference, his dresser – lending the film a different kind of theatrical realisation to that attained in Levring's film. The theatrical moments in *The Dresser* are staged performances and the film's connections with the *Lear* text are written into both its narrative and its character constructs; in *The King is Alive* it is the language of the *Lear* text, filtered through Henry's memory and connecting with this random collection of characters in a more private manner, that establishes its intertextual engagement with *King Lear*.

Levring's literary conceit also mirrors the performance mode of the Elizabethan and Jacobean stage in a way that Yates' film does not. The barren desert functions as a blank canvas similar to that provided by the open spaces of the Elizabethan and Jacobean stage and Levring's characters emulate the Elizabethan and Jacobean mode of stage production. Tiffany Stern notes that in both eras the lines of each actor were written onto separate rolls and given in isolation.[211] Here, it is Henry, former actor turned Holly-

[211] Tiffany Stern, *Rehearsal From Shakespeare to Sheridan* (Oxford:Clarendon Press, 2000), p. 10.

wood script-reader, who takes on the role of actor/manager, reproducing the play from memory and redistributing the lines to suit the people he has to work with, and it is his predicament, as an ageing man who has lost his daughter, that in part preordains the choice of *King Lear* as the play they are to perform. As he looks upon Charles practising his golf swing and the elderly, alcoholic American performing a jig against the backdrop of the desert wilderness, he recalls lines from *King Lear*, reciting 'Is man no more than this?' and acknowledging the parallels between the absurdity of their situation and that of the characters caught up in Shakespeare's narrative. Henry sees both as performing a 'fantastic striptease act of basic human needs' and proceeds to reconstruct Shakespeare's text from memory, his act of textual recreation echoing that of Godard's Shakespeare Junior and emulating the practice of remembering and recording Shakespeare's works, post-performance, in the Quarto and Folio editions of his plays.

For Levring the play-within-a-play narrative strategy allows him to explore the inner psyche of his characters. However, by revolving his drama around what may be construed as a contrived literary conceit, Levring is in danger of turning the film into the kind of intellectual *exercise* he claims to abhor'.[212] Taking the Dogme manifesto to heart, Amy Scott-Douglass holds the film up as a shining example of this Danish new wave's 'critical stance against Hollywood';[213] she cites Henry's transcription of Shakespeare's lines onto the back of a Hollywood blockbuster script titled *Space Killers* as 'a metaphor for Levring's dogmatic desire to replace Hollywood

[212] Levring in Kelly, pp. 213–214.

[213] Amy Scott-Douglass, 'Dogme Shakespeare 95: European Cinema, Anti-Hollywood Sentiment and the Bard', in *Shakespeare the Movie II: Popularising the Plays on Film, Television and DVD*, edited by Richard Burt and Lynda Boose (London and New York: Routledge, 2003), p. 253.

junk with good films',[214] rather than seeing it as a light-hearted jibe at Hollywood's expense. Scott-Douglass sees the film text as a statement about the current state of cinema: Gina represents both the vacuous stupidity of the Hollywood system and its audience whilst Catherine represents European cinema since she embodies 'the correct approach to art and a natural affinity to Shakespeare'.[215] But such a reading of the film text is incredibly flawed. It smacks of the kind of cultural elitism supposedly abhored by Levring and his Dogme 'brothers' and reduces characterisation to a purely conceptual level, negating the dramatic energies found in both Shakespeare's *King Lear* and Levring's film. Gina may be portrayed initially as an empty-headed, American tourist but Levring's development of her character as an increasingly vulnerable and self-sacrificing Cordelia figure is engineered to evoke our sympathies and she emerges as a much more likeable individual than the distanced, intellectual Catherine who, guilty of poisoning Gina, is ultimately aligned with the murderous Goneril.

In *The King is Alive* Levring interrogates the role of language and the very act of storytelling, mirroring Shakespeare's preoccupation with character development and language as the mainstay of the storyteller's art. Martha Nochimson argues that narrative is recast by Levring, taking it beyond the confines of 'ordinary plot'[216] and into the realms of what she terms 'a continuous, collaborative, spontaneous, humanising act of narrative'. Narrative becomes the 'catalytic agent' used to explore 'complex communal processes'.[217] Kanana, as narrator of the travellers' tale, takes on a chorus-like function; the film opens with an aerial shot of the desert sky, and

214 Ibid., p. 259.

215 Ibid., p. 260.

216 Martha Nochimson, 'The King Is Alive', *Film Quarterly* 55.2 (2001), pp. 52–54.

217 Ibid., pp. 52–54.

Kanana's voice-over, spoken in his native language and translated into subtitles, establishes an immediate sense of both the foreignness of the landscape and his role as storyteller. Visually, the frame focuses on an indistinct image of headlights approaching as he tells of 'strangers full of fear coming out of the desert', as if from nowhere, lending the moment a fable-like quality and signalling to the audience the commencement of a story filtered through his memory, his language and his cultural perspective rather than from the Western narrative viewpoint of the travellers involved in the tale, or from the Western tradition of tragedy with which *King Lear* is associated. It is the process of narration which becomes all important in this film, conventional narrative momentum being sidelined to such an extent that the arrival of rescuers who signal survival – and thus closure for this survival narrative – goes unheeded by the stranded travellers who continue to recite lines from *King Lear* over the poisoned Gina's funeral pyre.

Immediately, the significance of storytelling is foregrounded and we are immersed in the comforting conventions of such an act. Our narrator is inevitably unreliable since he tells of moments he cannot possibly have had access to, but we are swept along with the power of his narration and we accept his version of events just as the travellers accept Henry's version of *King Lear*. Levring reinforces the notion that storytelling is an essentially comforting process when Gina insists that Catherine tell her a tale in French: despite her incapacity to comprehend the language Gina finds the shared act of narration soothing, even though, ironically, Catherine's tale is about the stupidity and ignorance of her fellow travellers, Gina in particular. Kanana's narration is minimalistic: his use of language is functional and direct, suggesting that the power of the narration here comes through memories reconfigured visually rather than orally and in some ways offering a commentary on the operational differences between the visual medium of film and the linguistic medium of oral storytelling and prose narratives.

The story closes with remembered scenes of the moving bus taken from the start of the narrative, as if they are being replayed in Kanana's mind. He concludes their story and the film with the lines 'They are not here now. They are gone', re-establishing the notion that they are the stuff of fable: transient and insubstantial, alive only for as long as we have storytellers to tell their tale, as is also true of the works of Shakespeare, recorded and printed after the era of their production. Here, Levring is engaging in ideas similar to those raised in Godard's *King Lear* where we are forced to examine our relationship with the Ur-texts of our cultural heritage, but Levring's *Kanana* is a much more credible cypher for the successful interrogation of this relationship than Godard's bizarre Professor Pluggy could ever be. His is a voice that stands outside Western culture, providing us with the kind of objective perspective Godard seeks, unsuccessfully, to construct through Pluggy, whose incoherent, inaudible ramblings defy belief and fail to connect at the level of emotion or intellect, narrative or ideology.

The one 'character' that persists beyond the confines of Kanana's remembered story is the landscape: it provides the film's opening and closing images and its capacity to endure invests it with a majestic presence similar to that afforded to the landscape in Akira Kurosawa's *Ran* or Grigori Kozintsev's *Korol Lir* in which the landscape takes on an almost choral function. A number of sequences throughout the film illustrate the silent beauty of the desert landscape. The opening sequence (employing an aerial shot and thus working against a fundamental Dogme edict which outlaws the use of expensive technology)[218] pitches the vastness

---

[218] Dogme Manifesto, Rule Three: the camera must be hand-held.

and the tranquillity of the desert against shots of confined, noisy spaces inside the travellers' dilapidated bus. In the closing sequence we cut to a silent five second panning shot of the empty desert, suggesting it remains undisturbed by the invasion of the once stranded travellers.

Characterised by its size and its silence, Levring's location emphasises one of the central problems explored in this film. The silences of the desert and the minimal narrative interjections of Kanana point to the redundancy of language as a means of effective communication. This discourse on the redundancy of language extends to the travellers. Kanana notes on various occasions that:

> They ate less and they spoke words. Together they said words.
> They still didn't say them to each other.

His commentary refers on one level to the Shakespearean verse each traveller is rehearsing, but it also serves as a commentary on their inability to use their own language to communicate and to connect with each other at this stage. We have a series of such double-edged commentaries played over his blurred and distorted memories of the travellers, one of which acknowledges not only his inability to understand their language but also their own incapacity to make sense of what they say: he states, 'I didn't understand a word they said. Nor did they'. By using the rehearsal mode in his screenplay, Levring creates added layers of meaning, leading us to question the redundancy of words spoken without any true under-standing of their import, be they the words of Shakespeare or our everyday vocabulary. Since Shakespeare's *King Lear* is a play which is notably preoccupied with the redundancy of language, Lear's reiteration of Cordelia's line, 'Nothing', reverberating throughout the text, Levring's decision to explore the role of language in his film text is particularly apt as is his decision to foreground the artificiality of the literary conceit he is employing as a means to character development. Critic Jennifer Bottinelli points out that, unlike other screened Shakespeare adaptations which employ the rehearsal mode, such as Pacino's *Looking for Richard* (1996), Levring's use of this theatrical premise 'works against the master narrative of Shakespeare', deconstructing and then reconstructing the text as 'a frenzied commentary on filial and spousal rivalry'.[219]

It is through Shakespeare's language rather than through their shared language that the travellers finally reach a point of self-realisation and communal connection. The travellers are encouraged by Henry to find their own meaning in the words, rather than to perform some highly theatrical version thereof, again echoing the sentiments expressed within Shakespeare's *Hamlet* as Hamlet speaks with the players about the art of acting. Levring says that Liz's line – 'I need to know something about who these people are' – is 'a classic comment you get from actors'. But through Henry, Levring argues that 'you have to find this in the words', and in so doing, 'find (yourself) in this text'.[220] Like Shakespeare Junior in Godard's *King Lear*, Henry operates as the prompter-conductor[221] noted as an essential component of the rehearsal process during the production of plays in Shakespeare's era. Henry tells Amanda, for example, to seek her own meaning in the verses spoken by the fool, urging her to 'Listen to what the fool has to say to (her)' and it is through learning to hear the truth behind these lines that she

[219] Jennifer Bottinelli, 'Watching *Lear*: Resituating the Gaze at the Intersection of Film and Drama in Kristian Levring's *The King Is Alive*', *Literature/Film Quarterly* 3.2 (2005), p. 102.
[220] Levring in Kelly, p. 213.
[221] Stern, p. 121.

gains the strength to speak out in her own voice, rejecting her bullying, racist husband:

> I don't know you anymore. We don't know each other. I always knew you were nothing special ... I just wanted a peaceful life. You're ridiculous.

The *Lear* text is not reconstructed in any precise manner. We hear only snippets from the play and the lines of *various* characters are at times spoken by one traveller; Liz, seemingly in role as Goneril, is also given Regan's lines. Similarly there is no chronological delivery of Shakespeare's lines: as Ray ambles out into the desert, in a suicidal frame of mind due to his wife's constant flaunting of her desire for Moses, he utters Kent's closing line – ' I have a journey, sir, shortly to go,/My master calls, I must not say no' (5.3: 320–321) – but then proceeds to recite lines at random, his mental instability reflected in his disjointed delivery.

Levring's use of the Shakespearean language, though severely edited and taken out of its original context, remains reverential; it leads us to examine its meaning in closer detail than adaptations which aim for fidelity and in so doing he gives greater prominence to Shakespeare's language than numerous, more faithful renditions. As his characters come to an understanding of Shakespeare's language in their own terms, they simultaneously come to an understanding of themselves: Shakespeare's language becomes the primary method of discourse, pitted against the silences of the desert landscape, the clipped narration of Kanana, the empty conversations of the English-speaking travellers. Levring believes the best thing about Dogme is its capacity to 'force the truth out of the characters and settings';[222] the best thing about Shakespeare's

222 Levring in Kelly, p. 217.

verse is its capacity to force out similar truths and by focusing on the meaning behind the words Levring constructs a film text which encapsulates more of the *essence* of the borrowed text than other screen adaptations that are overly preoccupied with either the visual recreation of the images conjured by Shakespeare's language, or with recreating the narrative template of *King Lear*.

Levring's character constructs form part of an intellectual puzzle for the audience: we engage in his reconstruction of Shakespeare's text, piecing together the lines and identifying character traits as we too learn to make meaning. Charles is typical of the complicated character constructs created by Levring: he is Gloucester, Lear, Edmund and Cordelia. His pride and his inability to communicate with his son, Paul, echo Gloucester's incompetent handling of filial relationships and there are traces of Lear in Charles' personality too. His bizarre declaration of love for the much younger Gina and his arrogant belief that she will automatically return that love echo both Lear's demands for displays of daughterly affection and the incestuous sexual subtext found in Shakespeare's *King Lear*. His pride, his preoccupation with ageing and losing power similarly underscore his Lear-like qualities, but the vulnerability he shares with Lear is overshadowed by the darker facets of his nature and it is Henry who embodies the more empathetic elements of Shakespeare's protagonist. Furthermore, when rejected, Charles' actions mirror those of Edmund whose capacity to humiliate women he more than equals: once rejected by Gina/Cordelia he urinates on her as she lies dying. His death combines aspects of Edmund's and Cordelia's demise. Like Cordelia, he is hanged at the close but his death, like that of Edmund, is a final act of wilful self-destruction. Both Charles and Edmund accept their fate, preparing for it in a ritualistic manner, the one donning his armour the other his shirt and tie. And as with Edmund, Charles' death is not acknowledged by the others, no heed being paid to the image of his corpse suspended above Gina's dead body.

Film critic Richard Kelly acknowledges that, though *The King is Alive* is a `kind of savage sitcom, encased in a brilliant but *vulnerable* literary conceit', it exudes `gravity and pathos'[223] when realised on screen. It invites us to engage with Shakespeare's verse on both an intellectual and an emotional plane, presenting us with an adaptation that takes us back to the abstractions of the Elizabethan stage on which the meaning behind the words held the truth to the drama performed on its boards, and back to narrative momentum that can be sustained without recourse to the expensive regalia of Hollywood film-making.

[223] Ibid., p. 209.

PART 4:
The afterlife ...

The afterlife of *King Lear*: recent developments in the visual medium

For some critics, celluloid Shakespeare in general is an inherently reductive enterprise: it closes down the complexities of the text, dilutes its metaphorical and linguistic energies, and fails in the fidelity stakes. For others, the reconfigured film texts provide fresh, invigorating reinventions of Shakespeare's works which connect with their contemporary audiences. Paying homage to the text does not necessitate its treatment as untouchable, immutable literary monument: dues paid, the relocated text must find a niche within its new market place, and should establish a sense of the cultural preoccupations of its own era of production. But what exactly constitutes Shakespeare on screen in a modern viewing context?

The current popularity of loose adaptations to the small screen is attested by the success of the BBC's *ShakespeaRe-Told* series broadcast in November 2005, and there is an ever-growing collection of performance-based pieces related to Shakespeare appearing on sites like YouTube. Posted on the site, for example, is a particularly interesting 'gangsta' version, *King Lear in the Hood;*[1]

 [1] *King Lear in the Hood, YouTube,* posted 1/6/2006 (4 mins, 25) accessed 10/1/08.

King Lear is given the low budget action treatment, its brief reoriented narrative focusing here on the youthful sons of the subplot rather than the ageing patriarchs of Shakespeare's play. As public access to performance space becomes more and more attainable, our definitions will continue to expand rather than contract and the vitality of what Douglas Lanier terms 'Shakespop'[2] will continue to breathe new life into Shakespeare's works. Macbeth is the token tragedy given a modern make-over in the BBC's ShakespeaRe-Told series, and Othello is reconfigured as a contemporary drama in Andrew Davies' TV adaptation for ITV in 2001, but King Lear – to its creative detriment, some would argue – has been afforded a more traditional treatment in British television productions,[3] leaving the US television adaptation, King of Texas (2002), as the only small-screen, modern take on the Lear story, despite its many and varied reincarnations as contemporary genre fare on the big screen.

Channel 4's commissioning editor of the arts, Jan Younghusband, was behind the latest screened Shakespeare project – a televised King Lear that took Trevor Nunn's recent and very traditional RSC production[4] to the small screen after a TV absence of ten years. Filmed at Pinewood Studios, Nunn's reverential production brings an ageing Sir Ian McKellen to the role of King Lear. Despite

[2] Douglas Lanier, Shakespeare and Modern Popular Culture. Oxford: Oxford University Press, 2002.

[3] TV productions include the BBC's 1948 version starring William Devlin, a 1953 production starring Orson Welles, an American production starring James Earl Jones in 1974, a Thames TV production starring Patrick McGee in 1976, Michael Horden's BBC King Lear in 1982, Laurence Olivier's 1983 production, and Richard Eyre's BBC production starring Ian Holm in 1998.

[4] Trevor Nunn's Royal Shakespeare Company King Lear was first performed at The Courtyard, Stratford-on-Avon in April 2007.

McKellen's recent cinema roles, most notably as Gandalf in the *Lord of the Rings* trilogy (2001, 2002, 2003) and Magneto in the *X-Men* trilogy (2000, 2003, 2006), McKellen is still regarded as part of the theatrical fraternity; his theatrical background and his belief in the 'primacy of the play'[5] dictate a certain type of approach to the playing of Lear. In an interview with *The Guardian*'s Charlotte Higgins before the Christmas Day broadcast of *King Lear*, McKellen claimed somewhat prophetically that 'If you didn't see (the play) on the stage, you're lucky, because you'll have a better seat than anybody ever did in the theatre'.[6] McKellen seems to suggest that the closeness of the stage rendition and its televised counterpart is a positive, but in following its theatrical configuration so meticulously, Nunn's televised version is unable to transcend its stage origins: it remains, on the whole, a recording of a stage play, and there is little attempt to relocate the production into the very different medium of television. McKellen argues that television is 'the smallest theatre of all, where the audience is closer, more privileged than in any other venue', its tele-visuals allowing for the same level of audience intimacy provided by stage spaces like the RSC's Courtyard, its unflinching focus upon performance and delivery of Shakespeare's verse making it a medium that 'Shakespeare was made for'.[7] However, unlike Richard Eyre's 1998 televised production of *King Lear* in which the fluidity afforded by the camera is exploited to telling effect, our viewing experience in relation to Nunn's production becomes 'pseudo-theatrical' rather than tele-visual, despite the heightened immediacy and intimacy

[5] Emma Brockes, interview with Sir Ian McKellen, 'Every Inch a King', *The Guardian*, 4 November, 2007.

[6] Charlotte Higgins, 'Ian McKellen's *King Lear* to ring in the Christmas cheer for Channel 4', *The Guardian*, 26 November, 2008.

[7] Ian McKellen, DVD commentary, *King Lear*, 2008.

afforded by the use of lensed close ups, reaction shots, and soliloquies delivered to camera. It remains, in McKellen's own words, 'a record of a stage performance',[8] and as such it brings nothing fresh to our reading of Shakespeare's play.

The most recently staged *King Lear*,[9] directed by Rupert Goold, takes a bold and experimental approach to the play. Set in the late seventies and opening with lines from a Margaret Thatcher speech, it incorporates musical moments – Pete Postlethwaite's Lear singing *My Way* whilst dividing his territories, the Fool launching into *Singin' in the Rain* during the storm scenes, pop music blaring out of the radio during the reconciliation scene – and knights transformed into football thugs. His production stands in direct contrast both to Nunn's rendition of the play, and to a minimalist *King Lear* that formed part of Dominic Dromgoole's 2008 season at The Globe. Dromgoole's casting of David Calder as King Lear presented the audience with an exceptionally empathetic portrayal of a king in crisis, Calder, according to Dromgoole, using his 'feminine qualit(ies)', and 'play(ing) it gently, in a very confused, moving way'[10] as a means to highlight the redemptive possibilities inscribed within the play text. Despite Goold's daring interventions and attempts to revitalise the play, his production received critical backlash whilst the more conservative (and in Dromgoole's theatrical realisation the more emotive and restorative) renditions of recent times received critical acclaim.

The most current screenplay adaptation of *King Lear* – a costume drama rendition written in 2000 by Harold Pinter and

[8] Ibid.

[9] *King Lear* was staged at The Everyman Theatre, Liverpool, November, 2008 as part of Liverpool's year as European Capital of Culture.

[10] Rhoda Koenig, 'Dominic Dromgoole: Shakespeare's rule-breaker', *The Independent*, 1 May, 2008.

destined to be directed for cinema by Tim Roth with finance from Film Four – remains out of production, the screenplay at present being consigned to the archives of the British Library. Set in twelfth century Britain it is an adaptation that stays close to Shakespeare's text, its fidelity resulting in a screenplay which reads more like an edited version of Shakespeare's verse than an exercise in transformation to the very different medium of film. Tellingly, if produced, it would be only the third feature length film version of *King Lear* that appropriates Shakespeare's verse; whilst Brook's 1971 *King Lear* presents us with a challenging, experimental exploration of Shakespeare's language, Brian Blessed's low budget 1999 adaptation attracted little critical attention, its appropriation of the verse resulting in a stilted and highly theatrical costume rendition of the play. Despite Roth's initial contention that *their* purpose was to create a film that did not present a similarly traditional reading of the *Lear* narrative,[11] Pinter's treatment of Shakespeare's text creates a script that envisages little more than that, which could in part explain its continued absence from the screen.

Lear is, however, experiencing a potential renaissance in the visual medium at present. In addition to Nunn's recently televised *Lear*, plans to produce a big budget Hollywood version of *King Lear* were unveiled at the Cannes Film Festival in 2008. With a proposed pre-production budget of $35 million, and a stellar cast in place – including Keira Knightley (Cordelia), Gwyneth Paltrow (Regan), Naomi Watts (Goneril), and Sir Anthony Hopkins (King Lear) – this *Lear* seemed destined to take us into new cinematic territory. Director Joshua Michael Stern's intention was to adopt both the language and the story structure of Shakespeare's play without major edits; he also planned to place the narrative within very

[11] Adam Dawtrey, 'Roth Tackles *King Lear*', *Variety*, January, 2000.

specific temporal and geographical frameworks, connected to 'a period in British history from which Tolkien took his inspiration'.[12] For the first time in the play's cinematic history, it seemed we were to be presented with a decidedly grand, costume drama *Lear* on screen which may, like the Branagh Shakespeares to date, have proved to be a great success with certain types of audience. The epic visual splendour of the battle scenes envisioned in this proposed Hollywood version (as with those already realised in the epic battle-fields of Kurosawa's *Ran*) promised to lend the film a capacity to revitalise the *Lear* myth for the twenty-first century cinema audience, just as Shakespeare revitalised it for his contemporary theatrical scene. Screen reworkings of Shakespeare's *King Lear should* open up the text to new and decidedly *filmic* possibilities.

Yet the play's resistance thus far to the kind of heritage cinematic reading Stern envisioned introduced a well-founded note of caution, and memories of an earlier Cannes announcement of the Cannon Group's plans to make a big budget film version of *King Lear*,[13] with noted director Jean-Luc Godard at the helm, immediately sent out prophetic echoes of its potential commercial doom. Despite the initial optimism surrounding the project, financiers Ruby Films have recently announced their withdrawal from the production.[14] Whether this is a response to worldwide recession or to

[12] 'Anthony Hopkins to Give us a *Lear*', *The Guardian*, 25 June, 2008.

[13] Brad Stevens 'The American Friend', *Senses of Cinema*. (At the Cannes Film Festival in May 1985, Jean-Luc Godard, novelist Norman Mailer and Menahem Golan of Cannon Films reputedly signed a 'contract on a napkin', agreeing to work together on production of a film version of Shakespeare's *King Lear*). Online: www.sensesofcinema.com/contents/07/44/tom-luddy-godard.html

[14] 'Planned Keira Knightley version of *King Lear* cancelled', *Telegraph*.co.uk, 26 February, 2009 . Online: www.telegraph.co.uk/news/newstopics/celebritynews

the announcement of a rival production, directed by Michael Radford and starring Al Pacino as King Lear, remains unclear. Radford, Pacino and producer Barry Navidi have already worked together to translate Shakespeare's *The Merchant of Venice* (2004) to the cinema screen. The film generated mixed responses but Pacino's earlier involvement in *Looking For Richard* (1996), which documented his investigation into the staging of Shakespeare's *Richard III*, garnered critical acclaim, and like McKellen and Hopkins, Pacino has reached a timely age when to take up this part seems fitting. His connection with the role of Lear is also established in cinematic terms and it will be interesting to see if Pacino draws upon this in his portrayal of Lear in Radford's film.[15] Like Stern, Navidi's intention is to produce a heritage rendition of the play, retaining Shakespeare's verse and staying 'true to its period'.[16] However, this could prove problematic since *King Lear*, unlike *The Merchant of Venice*, is a text that continues to defy historical or geographical periodisation.

Adaptation: the debate goes on

According to Ramona Wray we are experiencing the 'advent of a Shakespeare on film boom' which brings with it a body of criticism that has become 'a discrete and increasingly canonical discipline.'[17] Whilst the boom is a positive, the inception of a discrete

---

[15] Like Shakespeare's Lear, Michael Corleone attempts to extricate himself from the burdens of leadership in both *The Godfather II* and *III*, and the tragic death of his Cordelia-like daughter in *The Godfather III* invites us to draw parallels between the plight of these two ageing patriarchs.

[16] Ben Child, 'Pacino to Play *King Lear* in New Film Adaptation', *The Guardian*, 4 February, 2009.

[17] Ramona Wray in *Shakespeare*, pp. 270–282.

and canonical discipline, generated to discuss a certain type of Shakespeare film, is not. At a time when the two disciplines of film and literature should be converging in their debate about screened Shakespeare, each seems to remain entrenched in its own academic area, each maintaining its own literary or filmic bias. In contrast to these discrete and canonical approaches, Daniel Rosenthal hints, in his recently published *One Hundred Shakespeare Films*, at the significance of Shakespeare and genre cinema and paves the way for a more academic exploration of the relationship between the two.[18] The codes and conventions offered by cinematic genres are of increasing significance to the screened Shakespeare industry: they provide cinematic shorthand for today's visually literate audiences, and offer supportive narrative networks for those unfamiliar with the 'source' text being translated to screen.

If cinematic Shakespeares are to continue to find a place in contemporary film markets, they must be responsive to the prevalent film industry climate and its multitude of influences; if analysers of these films are to examine fully the relationship between Shakespeare's play texts and the films which adapt or appropriate elements of them, they too must be responsive to the multitude of intertexts at work in production of the finished film product. Rather than focusing on readings which are driven by a narrow scholarly agenda of a filmic or a literary persuasion, we should aim for convergence of the two fields of enquiry, moving away from auteur-driven debates and matters relating to the primacy of so-called literary source texts, both of which entail a narrow, elitist approach to the study of screened Shakespeare.

---

[18] Daniel Rosenthal, *One Hundred Shakespeare Films* (London: BFI, 2007.)

Select bibliography

Ackroyd, Peter. 'Review: *Ran*', *The Spectator*, 15 March, 1986: 37.

Altman, Rick. *Film/Genre* (BFI Publishing: London, 1999).

Altman, Rick. *Sound Theory, Sound Practice* (Routledge: New York, 1992).

Anderegg, Michael. *Cinematic Shakespeare* (Rowman & Littlefield: London, 2004).

Andrew, Dudley. *Major Film Theories: An Introduction* (Open University Press: Maidenhead, 1976).

Atkinson, Michael. 'Crossing the Frontiers', *Sight & Sound* 1, 1994: 14–18.

Ball, Robert Hamilton. *Shakespeare on Silent Film: A Strange Eventful History* (George Allen and Unwin Ltd: London, 1968).

Barthes, Roland. *Image-Music-Text*, ed. and trans. S. Heath (Fontana/Collins: Glasgow, 1977).

Bennett, Susan. 'Godard and *Lear*: Trashing the Can(n)on', *Theatre Survey* 39.1, 1998: 7–19.

Berlin, Normand. 'Peter Brook's Interpretation of *King Lear*: "Nothing Will Come of Nothing"', *Literature/Film Quarterly* 15, 1977: 299–303.

National Film Theatre Translation of *Korol Lir*. *King Lear: After Shakespeare's Tragedy* (BFI Special Collections: BFI, London).

Billington, Michael. 'Review: Tierno Bokar', *The Guardian*, 2 June, 2005, http://arts.guardian.co.uk/critic/review (30/6/05).

Billson, Anne, 'The Emperor', *Time Out*, 12 March, 1986: 14.

Bluestone, George. (1957) *Novels into Film* (University of California Press: Berkeley, repr. 1973).

Bond, Edward. *Lear* (Methuen Publishing Ltd: London, 1983).

Bordwell, David. 'The Art Cinema as a Mode of Film Practice', *Film Criticism* 4.1, 1979: 56–64.

Bordwell, David and Thompson, Kirsten. Eds. (2nd ed. McGraw-Hill: London, Boston, MA, 2003).

Bottinelli, Jennifer. 'Watching *Lear*: Resituating the Gaze at the Intersection of Film and Drama in Kristian Levring's *The King is Alive*', *Literature/ Film Quarterly* 33.2, 2005: 101–109.

Bradley, A.C. *Shakespearean Tragedy: Lectures on Hamlet, Othello, King Lear and Macbeth*, 2nd ed. (Macmillan: London, 1905).

Bradshaw, Peter. 'Review: *My Kingdom*', *The Guardian*, 11 October, 2002, http://film.guardian.co.uk/News_Story/Critic_Review/Guardian_review (23/9/06).

Braudy, Leo and Cohen, Marshall. Eds. *Film Theory and Criticism*, 6th ed. (Oxford University Press: Oxford, 2004).

Brockes, Emma. 'Every Inch a King', *The Guardian*, 4 November, 2007.

Brook, Peter. *The Empty Space* (Harmondsworth Penguin: London, 1972).

Brook, Peter. *Draft Shooting Script: King Lear*, 9 September, 1968. (reprod. by The Folger Library: Washington DC).

Brook, Peter. *Second Draft Shooting Script: King Lear*, 5 December, 1968. (reprod. by The Folger Library: Washington DC).

Brook, Peter. 'Finding Shakespeare on Film', *Tulane Drama Review* 11.1, Fall, 1996: 117–121.

Browne, Nick. Ed. *Refiguring American Film Genres: Theory and History* (University of California Press: Berkeley, 1998).

Burch, Noël. *To the Distant Observer: Form and Meaning in the Japanese Cinema* (Scolar Press: London, 1979).

Burnett, Mark Thornton and Wray, Ramona. Eds. *Shakespeare, Film, Fin de Siècle* (Houndsmill: Macmillan Press Ltd, 2000).

Burnett, Mark Thornton and Wray, Ramona. Eds. *Screening Shakespeare in the Twenty-First Century* (Edinburgh University Press: Edinburgh, 2006).

Burt, Richard. *Unspeakable ShaXXXspeares: Queer Theory and American Kiddie Culture* (St Martin's Press: New York, 1998).

Burt, Richard and Boose, Lynda. Eds. *Shakespeare the Movie: Popularising the Plays on Film, TV, Video and DVD* (Routledge: London and New York, 1997).

Burt, Richard and Boose, Lynda. Eds. *Shakespeare the Movie II: Popularising the Plays on Film, TV, Video and DVD* (Routledge: London and New York, 2003).

Cahir, Linda, Costanzo. *Literature into Film: Theory and Practical Approaches* (McFarland: Jefferson, NC, 2006).

Carlson, Susan and Whitaker, Faye. 'Play to Novel to Film: An Interview with Jane Smiley on Rewriting Shakespeare', *Flyway* 5.1/2, 1999: 143–167.

Carroll, Noël. *The Philosophy of Horror or Paradoxes of the Heart* (Routledge: New York and London, 1990).

Cartelli, Thomas and Katherine Rowe. Eds. *New Wave Shakespeare on Screen* (Blackwell: Oxford, 2007).

Cartmell, Deborah. *Interpreting Shakespeare on Screen* (Macmillan: Basingstoke, 2000).

Cartmell, Deborah. 'Film as the New Shakespeare and Film on

Shakespeare: Revising the Shakespeare/Film Trajectory,'
Literature Compass 3/5, 2006: 1150–1159.

Cartmell, Deborah and Whelehan, Imelda. Eds. *Adaptations: From Text to Screen, Screen to Text* (Routledge: London and New York, 1999).

Cartmell, Deborah and Whelehan, Imelda. Eds. *The Cambridge Companion to Literature on Screen* (Cambridge University Press: Cambridge, 2007).

Chibnall, Steve and Murphy, Robert. Eds. *British Crime Cinema* (Routledge: London and New York, 1999).

Chibnall, Steve and Petley, Julian. Eds. *British Horror Cinema* (Routledge: London, 2002).

Child, Ben. 'Pacino to Play King Lear in New Film Adaptation', *The Guardian*, 4 February, 2009.

Chumo, Peter. 'Script Comments', *Creative Screenwriting* 8. 4, 2001: 20–22.

Church-Gibson, Pamela and Hill, John, Eds. *The Oxford Guide to Film Studies* (Oxford University Press: Oxford 1998).

Cohan, Steve and Hark, Ina Rae. Eds. *The Road Movie Book* (Routledge: London, 1997).

Cohn, Ruby. 'The Triple Action Theatre Group', *Theatre Journal* 27.1, 1975: 56–62.

Collick, John. *Shakespeare, Cinema and Society* (Manchester University Press: Manchester, 1989).

Coppola, Francis Ford and Puzo, Mario. *The Godfather: Screenplay* (3rd draft, March, 1971), www.awesomefilm.com/script/THEGODFATHER.txt (8/9/06).

Coppola, Francis Ford and Puzo, Mario. *The Godfather Part II: Screenplay* (2nd Draft, Sept. 1973), www.awesomefilm.com/script/godfather2 (8/9/06).

Coppola, Francis Ford and Puzo, Mario. *The Godfather Part III:*

Screenplay, www.awesomefilm.com/script/godfather2 (8/9/06).

Corrigan Timothy. Ed. *Film and Literature: An Introduction and a Reader* (Prentice Hall: New Jersey, 1999).

Creed, Barbara. *The Monstrous Feminine: Film, Feminism, Psychoanalysis* (Routledge: London, 1993).

Davies, Anthony. *Filming Shakespeare's Plays: The Adaptations of Olivier, Welles and Kurosawa* (Cambridge University Press: Cambridge, 1990).

Davies, Anthony and Wells, Stanley. *Shakespeare and the Moving Image* (Cambridge University Press: Cambridge, 1999).

Dawtrey, Adam. 'Roth tackles *King Lear*', *Variety*, January 2000.

Desmond, John and Hawkes, Peter. *Adaptation: Studying Film and Literature* (McGraw-Hill: Boston, MA, 2006).

Dogme95, http://www.dogme95.dk (10/10/06).

Dollimore, Jonathan and Sinfield, Alan. Eds *Political Shakespeare: New Essays in Cultural Materialism* (Manchester University Press: Manchester, 1985).

Donaldson, Peter. *Shakespearean Films/Shakespearean Directors* (Unwin Hyman, Inc.: Mass., London, 1990).

Ebert, Roger. 'Review: *A Thousand Acres*', *Chicago Sunday Times,* 19 September. 1997, http://rogerebert.suntimes.com (23/9/06).

Eckert, Charles. *Focus on Shakespeare's Films* (Prentice-Hall Inc.: New Jersey, 1972).

Elliot, Kamilla. *Rethinking the Novel/Film Debate* (Cambridge University Press: Cambridge, 2007).

Escher , Edward. Ed. *Shakespeare and his Contemporaries in Performance* (Ashgate: Aldershot, 2000).

Falcon, Richard. 'Magnificent Obsession', *Sight and Sound* 13: 3, 2003: 12–15.

Ferguson, Margaret, Quilligan, Maureen and Vickers, Nancy. Eds. *Rewriting the Renaissance: The Discourses of Sexual Difference in Early Modern Europe* (The University of Chicago Press: London, 1986).

Foakes, R.A. 'Performance Theory and Textual Theory: A Retort Courteous', *Shakespeare* 2:1, 2006: 47–58.

French, Emma. *Selling Shakespeare to Hollywood: the Marketing of Filmed Shakespeare Adaptations from 1989 to the New Millennium* (University of Hertfordshire Press: Herts, 2006).

Gardaphé, Fred L. *From Wiseguys to Wisemen: The Gangster and Italian American Masculinities* (Routledge: New York, London, 2006).

Genette, Gérard. *Narrative Discourse: an Essay in Method,* trans. Jane Lewin (Cornell University Press: Ithaca, New York, 1980).

Gever, Martha, Greyson, John, and Parmar, Praibha. Eds. *Queer Looks: Perspectives on Lesbian and Gay Film and Video* (Routledge: New York, 1993).

Giddings, Robert and Sheen, Erica. Eds. *The Classic Novel From Page to Screen* (Manchester University Press: Manchester, 2000).

Goodwin, James. *Akira Kurosawa and Intertextual Cinema* (John Hopkins University Press: Baltimore, 1994).

Graffy, Julian, Iodanova, Dina, Taylor, Richard and Wood, Nancy. Eds. *BFI Companion to Eastern European and Russian Cinema* (BFI Publishing: London, 2000).

Grant, Barry Keith. Ed. *The Dread of Difference: Gender and the Horror Film* (University of Texas Press: Austin, 1996).

Grieveson, Lee, Sonnet, Esther and Stanfield, Peter. Eds. *Mob Culture: Hidden Histories of the American Gangster* Film (Berg: Oxford, 2002).

Hammond, Michael and Williams, Ruth. Eds. *Contemporary American Cinema* (Open University Press: Maidenhead, 2006).

Hatchuel, Sarah. *Shakespeare, from Stage to Screen* (Cambridge University Press: Cambridge, 2004).

Hawkins, Harriet. *Classics and Trash: Traditions and Taboos in High Literature and Popular Modern Genres* (Harvester Wheatsheaf: Hemel Hempstead, 1990).

Hayman, Ronald. 'Interview with director Grigori Kozintsev', *Transatlantic Review* Vol. Summer, 1973: 10–15.

Henderson, Diane E. Ed. *A Concise Companion to Shakespeare on Screen* (Blackwell Publishing Limited: Malden, Oxford, Victoria, 2006).

Higgins, Charlotte. 'Ian McKellen's *King Lear* to ring in the Christmas cheer for Channel 4', *The Guardian*, 26 November, 2008.

Higson, Andrew. *Waving the Flag: Constructing a National Cinema in Britain* (Clarendon Press: Oxford, 1995).

Hill, Jonathan and Church-Gibson, Pamela. *The Oxford Guide to Film Studies* (Oxford University Press: Oxford, 1998).

Hirsh, Foster. DVD commentary, *House of Strangers*, 2006.

Holderness, Graham. *Visual Shakespeare: Essays in Film and Television* (University of Hertfordshire Press: Herts, 2002).

Holderness, Graham. 'Shakespeare Rewound', *Shakespeare Survey* 45, 1992: 64.

Holland, Peter. Ed. *Shakespeare Survey 55: King Lear and its Afterlife* (Cambridge University Press: Cambridge, 2002).

Howlett, Kathy. *Framing Shakespeare on Film* (Ohio University Press: Ohio, 2000).

Hutcheon, Linda. *A Theory of Adaptation* (Routledge: London and New York, 2006).

Impastato, David. 'Godard's *Lear.* Why is it so bad?' *Shakespeare Bulletin* 12:3, 1994: 38–41.

Jackson, Russell. Ed. *The Cambridge Companion to Shakespeare on Film* (Cambridge University Press: Cambridge, 2000).

Jones, Darryl. *Horror: A Thematic History in Fiction and Film* (Arnold: London, 2002).

Jorgens Jack. *Shakespeare on Film* (Indiana University Press: London and Bloomington, 1977).

Kane, Julie. 'From the Baroque to Wabi: Translating Animal Imagery from Shakespeare's *King Lear* to Kurosawa's *Ran*', *Literature/Film Quarterly* 25, 1997: 146–151.

Kelly, Richard. *The Name of the Book is Dogme95* (Faber & Faber: London, 2000).

Kitses, Jim. *Horizons West* (Thames and Hudson Limited: London, 1969).

Klein, M. and Parker, G. Eds. *The English Novel and the Movies* (Frederick Ungar: New York, 1981).

Koenig, Rhoda. 'Dominic Dromgoole: Shakespeare's rule-breaker', *The Independent*, 1 May, 2008.

Kott, Jan. *Shakespeare Our Contemporary* (Routledge: London, 1967).

Kozintsev, Grigori. *King Lear, the Space of Tragedy: The Diary of a Film Director* (University of California Press: Berkeley, 1977).

Kozintsev, Grigori. *Shakespeare: Time and Conscience* (Dobson: London, 1967).

Kurosawa, Akira, Oguni, Hideo and Masato, Ide. *Ran* (Shambala: Boston and London, 1986).

Langford, Barry. *Film Genre: Hollywood and Beyond* (Edinburgh University Press: Edinburgh, 2005).

Lanier, Douglas. *Shakespeare and Modern Popular Culture* (Oxford University Press: Oxford, 2002).

Lanier, Douglas. 'Shakespeare and Cultural Studies: An Overview', *Shakespeare* 2:2, 2006: 228–248.

LaSalle Mick, 'Review: "*Acres*" Bogs Down Despite Grand Cast', *San Francisco Chronicle*, 15 September, 1997.

Lehmann Courtney. *Shakespeare Remains: Theatre to Film, Early Modern to Postmodern* (Cornell University Press: Ithaca and London, 2002).

Leitch, Thomas. 'Adaptation Studies at a Crossroads'. *Adaptation* 1:1, 2008: 63–77.

Leitch, Thomas. *Film Adaptation and Its Discontents: From Gone With the Wind to The Passion of the Christ* (The John Hopkins University Press: Baltimore, 2007).

Lothe, Jakob. *Narrative in Fiction and Film* (Oxford University Press: Oxford, 2000).

Mack, Maynard. *King Lear in Our Time* (Methuen: London, 1966).

Maerz, Jessica. 'Godard's *King Lear.* Referents Provided Upon Request', *Literature/Film Quarterly* 32.2, 2004: 108–114.

Manvell, Roger. *Shakespeare and the Film* (J.M. Dent & Sons: London, 1971).

Marowitz, Charles. *Recycling Shakespeare* (Macmillan: London, 1991).

McCabe, Colin. *The Eloquence of the Vulgar: Language, Cinema and the Politics of Culture* (BFI Publishing: London, 1999).

McDonald, Keiko. *Japanese Classical Theatre in Films* (Associated University Presses: London, 1994).

McFarlane, Brian. *Novel to Film: An Introduction to the Theory of Adaptation* (Clarendon Press: Oxford, 1996).

McKee, Robert. *Story: Substance, Structure, Style, and the Principles of Screenwriting* (Methuen: London, 1999).

Metz, Christian. *Film Language: A Semiotics of the Cinema*, trans. Michael Taylor (Oxford University Press: New York, 1974).

Mulvey, Laura. 'Visual Pleasure and Narrative Cinema', *Screen* 16.3, 1975: 6–18.

Murphy, Robert. *Sixties British Cinema* (BFI Publishing: London, 1992).

Murphy, Robert. Ed. *The British Cinema Book* (2nd edition) (BFI Publishing: London, 2001).

Naremore, James. *Film Adaptation* (The Athlone Press: London, 2000).

Naremore, James. *More Than Night: Film Noir in its Contexts* (University of California: Berkeley, Los Angeles, London, 1998).

Neale, Steve. *Genre* (BFI Publishing: London, 1983).

Neale, Steve. Ed. *Genre and Contemporary Hollywood* (BFI Publishing: London, 2002).

Nicoll, Allardyce. *Film and Theatre* (Harrap & Company Ltd: London, 1936).

Nochimson, Martha. 'The King is Alive', *Film Quarterly* 55.2, 2001: 48–54.

Nowell-Smith, Geoffrey. '*Paris-Match*: Godard and Cahiers', *Sight and Sound* 11:6, 2001: 18–21.

Ogden, James and Scouten, Arthur. Eds. *Lear: From Study to Stage* (Associated University Presses: London, 1997).

Powrie, Phil. 'Godard's "*Prenom: Carmen*", Masochism and the Male Gaze', *Forum for Modern Language Studies* 31:1, 1995: 64.

Powrie, Phil. *French Cinema in the 1980s: Nostalgia and the Crisis of Masculinity* (Clarendon Press: Oxford, 1997).

Prince, Stephen. T*he Warrior's Camera: The Cinema of Akira Kurosawa* (Princeton University Press: Princeton, New Jersey, 1999).

Puzo, Mario. *The Godfather* (Heineman: London, 1969).

Raban, Jonathan. 'Review: Brook's *King Lear*', *New Statesman*, 30 July, 1971: 15.

Richie, Donald. *Japanese Cinema: Film, Style and National Character* (Anchor: New York, 1971).

Rimmon-Kenan, Shlomith. *Narrative Fiction: Contemporary Poetics* (Routledge: London, 1999).

Roman, Shari. *Digital Babylon: Hollywood, Indiewood & Dogme 95* (Lone Eagle Publishing Company: California, 2001).

Romney, Jonathan. 'Overruled (Dogme 95 Film Festival, Cannes, France)', *New Statesman*, 4 October, 1999, http://www.findarticles.com/cf (21/10/01).

Rosenbaum, Jonathan. 'Theory and Practice: the Criticism of Jean-Luc Godard', *Sight and Sound* 41:3, 1972: 124.

Rosenthal, Daniel. 'The Bard on Screen', *The Guardian*, 7 April 2007, http://film.guardian.co.uk/features/featurespage (17/4/07).

Rosenthal, Daniel. *100 Shakespeare Films* (BFI Publishing: London, 2007).

Rothwell, Kenneth. *A History of Shakespeare on Screen: A Century of Film and Television* (Neal-Schuman: London, 1990).

Rothwell, Kenneth. *A History of Shakespeare on Screen* (Cambridge University Press: Cambridge, 1999).

Rundle, Peter. 'An Aesthetic Choice', an interview with Kristian Levring, 10 November, 1999, www.dogme95.dk/news/interview/levring_interview.htm (5/8/06).

Rutter, Carol C. *Enter The Body: Women and Representation on Shakespeare's Stage* (Routledge: London, 2001).

Saunders, John. *The Western Genre: From Lordsburgh to Big Whiskey* (Wallflower Press: London, 2001).

Schatz, Thomas. *Hollywood Genres: Formulas, Film-making and the Studio System* (McGraw-Hill: New York, 1981).

Schneider, Steven Jay and Shaw, Daniel. Eds. *Dark Thoughts: Philosophic Reflections on Cinematic Horror* (The Scarecrow Press: Maryland and Oxford, 2003).

Schumacher, Michael. *Francis Ford Coppola: A Film-maker's Life* (Bloomsbury: New York, 1999).

Serper, Zvilca. 'Lady Kaede In Kurosawa's *Ran*: Verbal and Visual Characterisation Through Animal Traditions', *Japan Forum* 13.2, 2001: 145–158.

Serper, Zvilca. 'Blood Visibility/Invisibility in Kurosawa's *Ran*', *Literature/Film Quarterly* 28.2, 2000: 149–154.

Shakespeare, William. *King Lear*. The Arden Shakespeare. Ed. R.A. Foakes (Thomas Nelson & Sons: London, 1997).

Sharrett, Christopher. *Crisis Cinema: The Apocalyptic Idea in Postmodern Narrative Film* (Maisonneuve Press: Washington DC, 1993).

Shaughnessy, Robert. Ed. *Shakespeare on Film*, (St Martin's Press: New York, 1998).

Singh, Anita. 'Keira Knightley to star in film Of *King Lear*', *The Telegraph*, 20 May, 2008.

Sinyard, Neil. *Filming Literature: The Art of Screen Adaptation* (Croom Helm: London, 1986).

Stam, Robert and Raengo, Alessandra. Eds. *Literature and Film: A Guide to the Theory and Practice of Film Adaptation* (Blackwell Publishing: Oxford, 2005).

Stern, Tiffany. *Rehearsal From Shakespeare to Sheridan* (Clarendon Press: Oxford, 2000).

Stevens, Brad. 'The American Friend', *Senses of Cinema*, www.sensesofcinema.com/contents/07/44/tom-luddy-godard.html (3/3/06).

Street, Sarah. *British National Cinema* (Routledge: London and New York, 1997).

Taylor, Richard. *BFI Companion to Eastern European Cinema and Russian Cinema* (BFI Publishing: London, 2000).

The Telegraph. 'Planned Keira Knightley version of *King Lear* cancelled', 26 February, 2009. www.telegraph.co.uk/news/newstopics/celebritynews

Thompson, Ann. 'Kurosawa's *Ran*: Reception and Interpretation', *East-West Film Journal* 3.2, 1989: 1–13.

Wagner, Geoffrey. *The Novel and Cinema* (Associated University Presses: Cranbury, 1975).

Walker, Alexander. *Hollywood, England: The British Film Industry in the Sixties* (Michael Joseph Ltd: London, 1974).

Warshow, Robert. Ed. *The Immediate Experience* (Atheneum: New York, 1970).

Welsh, James, Vela, Richard and Tibbetts, John. *Shakespeare Into Film* (Checkmark Books: New York, 2002).

Wells, Stanley, and Taylor, Gary. Eds. *The Complete Oxford Shakespeare* (Oxford University Press: Oxford, 1986).

Wilds, Lillian. 'One *King Lear* for Our Time: A Bleak Film Vision by Peter Brook', *Literature/Film Quarterly* 4, 1976: 159–164.

Willson Jr, Robert F. *Shakespeare in Hollywood: 1929–1956* (Associated University Presses: New Jersey, 2000).

Wilson Knight, G. *The Wheel of Fire: Interpretations of Shakespearean Tragedy* (Methuen: London, 1949).

Woll, Josephine. *Real Images: Soviet Cinema and the Thaw* (I.B. Taurus Publishers: London, New York, 2000).

Wollen, Peter. 'Godard and Counter Cinema: *Vent D'Est*', *Afterimage* (Visual Studies Workshop, Autumn, 1972): 7–16.

Wray, Ramona. 'Shakespeare on Film in the New Millennium', *Shakespeare* 3.2, 2007: 270–282.

Yoshimoto, Mitsuhiro. *Kurosawa, Film Studies and Japanese Cinema* (Duke University Press: Durham NC, 2000).

Select filmography

....

All That Heaven Allows, USA, directed by Douglas Sirk, 1955.

A Thousand Acres, USA, directed by Jocelyn Moorhouse, 1997.

Bonnie and Clyde, USA, directed by Arthur Penn, 1967.

Broken Arrow, USA, directed by Delmer Daves, 1950.

Broken Lance, USA, directed by Edward Dmytryk. 1954.

Butch Cassidy and the Sundance Kid, USA, directed by George
   Roy Hill, 1969.

Devil's Doorway, USA, directed by Anthony Mann, 1951.

Easy Rider, USA, directed by Dennis Hopper, 1969.

Festen, Denmark/Sweden, directed by Thomas Vinterberg, 1998.

Hamlet, UK, directed by Kenneth Branagh, 1996.

Hamlet, USA, directed by Michael Almereyda, 2000.

High Noon, USA, directed by Fred Zinnemann, 1952.

House of Strangers, USA, directed by Joseph L. Mankiewicz, 1949.

Julius Caesar, UK, directed by Stuart Burge, 1970.

King Lear, UK, directed by Peter Brook, 1971.

King Lear, UK, directed by Steve Rumbelow, 1976.

King Lear, USA, directed by Jean-Luc Godard, 1987.

King Lear (TV), UK, directed by Richard Eyre, 1998.

King Lear, UK, directed by Brian Blessed, 1999.

King Lear (TV), UK, directed by Trevor Nunn, 2008.

King of Texas (TV), USA, directed by Uli Edel, 2002.

Korol Lir, Soviet Union, directed by Grigori Kozintsev, 1970.

Macbeth, USA, directed by Roman Polanski, 1971.

My Kingdom, UK, directed by Don Boyd, 2001.

Ran, Japan/ France, directed by Akira Kurosawa, 1985.

The Dresser, UK, directed by Peter Yates, 1983.

The Godfather, USA, directed by Francis Ford Coppola, 1972.

The Godfather Part II, USA, directed by Francis Ford Coppola, 1974.

The Godfather Part III, USA, directed by Francis Ford Coppola, 1990.

The Grapes of Wrath, USA, directed by John Ford, 1940.

The King is Alive, Sweden/ Denmark/ USA, directed by Kristian Levring, 2000.

The Searchers, USA, John Ford, 1955.

The Wizard of Oz, USA, directed by Victor Fleming, 1939.

William Shakespeare's Romeo and Juliet, USA, directed by Baz Luhrmann, 1996.

Written on the Wind, USA, directed by Douglas Sirk, 1956.

Index

••